BROTHER JIMMY'S® BBQ

MORE THAN 100 RECIPES
FOR PORK, BEEF, CHICKEN & THE ESSENTIAL SOUTHERN SIDES

JOSH LEBOWITZ, OWNER  WITH EVA PESANTEZ & SEAN EVANS

FOOD PHOTOGRAPHY BY LUCY SCHAEFFER

STEWART, TABORI & CHANG | NEW YORK

PUBLISHED IN 2012 by Stewart, Tabori & Chang
An imprint of ABRAMS

Library of Congress Cataloging-in-Publication Data
Lebowitz, Josh.
Brother Jimmy's BBQ : more than 100 recipes for pork, beef, chicken, and the essential southern sides / Josh Lebowitz, Eva Pesantez.
  p. cm.
 ISBN 978-1-58479-954-2 (pbk.)
1. Barbecuing. I. Pesantez, Eva. II. Title.
 TX840.B3L43 2012
 641.7'6—dc23

2011036181

EDITOR: Natalie Kaire
DESIGNER: Laura Palese
PRODUCTION MANAGER: Tina Cameron
FOOD STYLIST: Simon Andrews
PROP STYLIST: Amy Williams

The text of this book was composed in Din, Cheap Pine, Cordoba, Stud, and Elephant.

Printed and bound in the U.S.A.

10 9 8 7 6 5 4 3 2 1

ABRAMS
THE ART OF BOOKS SINCE 1949

115 West 18th Street
New York, NY 10011
www.abramsbooks.com

BROTHER JIMMY'S® BBQ

MORE THAN 100 RECIPES
FOR PORK, BEEF, CHICKEN & THE ESSENTIAL SOUTHERN SIDES

BROTHER JIMMY'S® BBQ

BBQ

MORE THAN 100 RECIPES

FOR PORK, BEEF, CHICKEN & THE ESSENTIAL SOUTHERN SIDES

CONTENTS

LETTER FROM JOSH

MY LOVE OF BARBECUE BEGAN IN COLLEGE, THE MINUTE I SET FOOT INSIDE REDBONES BARBECUE RESTAURANT IN SOMERVILLE, MASSACHUSETTS.

It was the first barbecue joint I'd ever been to, and I thought it was amazing. Walking in, the scent of the hickory oak was so potent and mouthwatering; it was one of those places where you knew in one whiff that everything would taste delicious. I dived into plates of ribs, pulled pork, mac and cheese, and mashed potatoes, each one as perfect as the last.

It was tucked away in this brick building on a side street, and it was always slammed with customers. You'd have to wait in line for an hour sometimes, that tantalizing smell pouring from their smokers, teasing you the whole time. When you were finally inside, it was loud, but not from the music. The din of happy people chattering away filled my ears, and I loved it. I enjoyed the action, the excitement, and the vibe of Redbones. And the ribs tasted fantastic. I was hooked on the whole experience.

Later, while on a cross-country trip to California my junior year, my friend and I drove through the heart of the South. As we wove our way through North Carolina, South Carolina, Tennessee, Mississippi, Georgia, Alabama, and Louisiana, we'd stop whenever possible to feast on barbecue, exploring every edible facet of Southern cuisine.

There is something undeniably familiar about a barbecue experience. Entering each restaurant was like setting foot into a home kitchen, a mythical incarnation of our mental ideals inspired by everything from the Waltons to our grandmother's home. Every time, it was warm and inviting, right down to the checkered cloths wrapping each table. Sure, the fare tastes different in each spot, but it's consistently rooted in the same concept: no-frills, deconstructed plates of comfort food, cooked to succulent perfection. Simply mix all the flavors into one big pile and dig in. The resulting bites are always delicious.

In the South, barbecue represents more than just a juicy pulled pork shoulder sandwich; barbecue below the Mason-Dixon was always about celebration. Before there was tailgating there was pig pickin', which can best be summed up as a gathering of friends around the slow cooking of a whole hog. Over time, these gatherings have grown and transformed into the traditional Southern barbecue we've all come to know. And though barbecue has evolved far past various savory pulled meats, the integral parts of a good pig pickin' or barbecue still remain the same: solid music, jubilant dancing, a healthy assortment of booze, good ole Southern hospitality, and—of course—sweet tea, extra heavy on the sweetness. Simple recipes mastered through years of experience combined with this carefree, fun environment provided the foundation for each of the restaurants I was lucky enough to enjoy on my travels.

As I wrapped up college, the innocuous seed of a life of barbecue had been planted in my mind. Simultaneously, New Yorkers got

their first taste of some South in their mouth when the doors of a small, ramshackle little restaurant opened in 1989 on the Upper East Side. Founded by Jimmy Goldman, Brother Jimmy's was created to be all about the legendary North Carolina slow-smokin' 'cue, where pork was liberally seasoned, rubbed, and then left atop smoldering hickory wood for half a day before being piled high onto a plate, served with all the country fixins. Brother Jimmy's went on to produce some of the finest barbecue ever to hit a New Yorker's plate (per the *New York Times* in a lauding review that proclaimed the arrival of true barbecue in NYC right after the opening).

When I began working for Jimmy in 1996, it was a cathartic moment: I realized that my passion for barbecue could forever become my profession. When I took ownership of Brother Jimmy's in 2000, the most important tenet I strived to adhere to was the fact that proper barbecue isn't just about food. It's an affair that encompasses everything good in life: family, friends, food, and fun, and at Brother Jimmy's we're proud to re-create that experience every day, from open to close, in each of our seven locations. It's the same essence I found in the Southern culture I'd seen years earlier, during tailgates, backyard barbecues, and some of the eateries I'd visited.

Any night at any Brother Jimmy's, you can find people dancing around, smiling, and generally enjoying life. Every night is a lovefest, with tables of strangers coming together, clinking Natural Light cans of brew, wrapping their arms around one another, and cheering on their favorite team or performing impromptu karaoke to the Allman Brothers. This vibe, this excitement, this feeling is what Brother Jimmy's is about. There's a reason *Zagat* ranked us among the top five nightspots in all of New York.

Because of all of this, Brother Jimmy's is more than just a barbecue house. We're a true Southern restaurant: We serve a diverse and robust selection of classics Southerners have come to love, and we just happen to serve some great authentic barbecue too. We believe in the North Carolina method of barbecue, which is that good 'cue is defined by the taste of the meat and not the sauce slathered atop it. I originally was misled in believing the sauce is the secret to barbecuing success, but any true Southerner can tell you the flavor of the meat is paramount, and we agree with that stance.

We're connoisseurs of the 'cue, just as our customers are connoisseurs of good food and good times. Only to the most initiated does it matter that we're serving Eastern-style barbecue (representing the eastern part of North Carolina). So while we can tell you that Eastern style is argued to be the original American barbecue—because it most closely resembles the way it was prepared in the

seventeenth century when whole hogs were roasted over pits with oak or hickory coals—or that true Eastern sauce contains no tomato extracts, presumably because early settlers believed tomatoes were poisonous, the only thing that really matters after slaving over a hot stove, smoker, or grill is that you find everything as delicious as possible. We'll not only show you how to arrive at that perfect end result; we'll also share some of our other country staples—from Country-Fried Steak (page 145) and Fried Chicken Breasts (page 160) to Cornmeal-Crusted Catfish Nuggets (page 87), Smoky Corn and Black Bean Chow Chow (page 212), Hush Puppies with Maple Butter (page 75), and even Fried Green Tomatoes (page 73)—that will perfectly round out your barbecues.

But what's the point of great food if the environment is off? After all, perception is everything. We work hard to create an ambiance that transports our guests down South as soon as they step through the doors of any Brother Jimmy's. The decor—ranging from flour and feed bags to old hubcaps and walls composed of old racecar tires—is authentically Southern, mostly purchased from salvage yards in North and South Carolina. Above all, we want that warm, casual, friendly atmosphere—one where contractions are in. Every time you leave, you'll hear one of our cheerful waitresses tell you, "Thanks for comin'!" And we wouldn't have it any other way.

The sum of all of these parts is that Brother Jimmy's is more than a restaurant or a bar, just as what you're holding in your hand right now is more than a cookbook. You're holding a small piece of our DNA, the blueprint to our success, which we're more than happy to share with you. If you're already a fan and customer at a Brother Jimmy's, you'll find all of our popular menu items, plus many new recipes that were created just for this cookbook. Here you'll find everything from sweet and spicy barbecue sauces to mac and cheese and our sliced brisket—recipes that have been passed down through generations of Southern folk and refined until they're absolutely perfect. All of it perfect for the entertainer in you.

Because the food is one of the more vital parts of the overall equation, we'll be including tips and tricks to elevate you from novice pit master to a seasoned veteran. We'll show you precisely how to turn your kitchen into a home version of ours, whether you live in an apartment, condo, or house. Unsure of which seasonings and spices are the best? We'll show you how to create amazing custom blends from scratch. We'll break down tried-and-true cooking techniques gleaned from more than two decades of producing top-notch barbecue and guide you on how to replicate the results with your grill, smoker, oven, or stove.

You've got to wash down scrumptious creations in true Southern style, so we've included all our favorite drink creations, including Louisville Lemonade (the Kentucky version of the whiskey-infused lemonade), our Bloody Beer (a Bloody Mary with beer instead of vodka), Palmetto Punch, Trash Can Punch, and Swamp Water—a fishbowl full of alcohol—for the party animal in you. We'll give you step-by-step directions on how to properly muddle a mint julep and how to cut and arrange your garnishes. We've even got tips on how to get a can of beer freezing cold in under four minutes (hint: salt water is involved).

But our blueprint delves well beyond our food and drinks. Just like we deconstruct each platter of deliciousness leaving our kitchen, this book is here to deconstruct a fun night steeped in Southern tradition, breaking it apart into the fundamental elements that have evolved since the days of pig pickin'. This book isn't here just to help you re-create our popular dishes in your kitchen; it's here to help you re-create the great vibe you experience at our establishments.

Because the soundtrack of barbecue is blues, country, and rock 'n' roll, we've got some starter playlists to share with you, directly from our restaurants. We believe that you should switch up the tempo every ten minutes, so these musical mixes will have you and your friends rocking into the wee hours of the morning. Our tunes are designed to get you out of your seat and dancing and fired up.

Peppering the whole book are quirky entertaining tidbits we've learned over the years, which never fail to spice up our restaurants and parties. Among the gems you'll find are some drinking games and how to play bags or cornhole, beer pong, and more. The information will run the gamut on topics, but it'll always be interesting.

In short, this book is all you'll need to bring a little Brother Jimmy's home to your rooftop cocktails, afternoon beach party, backyard barbecue, Sunday tailgate, or any other event you can imagine. Obviously, if you want to cook dinner for two, the recipes are perfect for that as well. My belief is that barbecue is supposed to be fun, and this book will outline many of the ways Brother Jimmy's has been making it fun for New Yorkers for more than twenty years.

READY TO PUT SOME SOUTH IN YOUR MOUTH? GOOD. LET'S GET STARTED!

JOSH LEBOWITZ, owner of Brother Jimmy's

INTRODUCTION
BASICS OF 'CUE

Plain and simple, Brother Jimmy's is the rare place up North to get the best barbecue without a trip to the South. Anyone looking for superb Southern food set to a blues, rock 'n' roll, and country soundtrack knows to head through our doors. Because of this, Brother Jimmy's means a good time, and we're here to show you how to re-create our environment right in your own home. You'll find everything from how to center the right foods around that big weekend rivalry sports bash you're throwing to how to mix the best cocktails that'll keep you and your guests partying through the afternoon or night. After all, barbecue is a social affair, encompassing Southern hospitality with a crew of family and friends and great eats.

LET'S FIRE UP THE GRILL AND CALL SOME PALS. IT'S BARBECUE TIME.

TOOLS OF THE TRADE & HOW TO USE THEM

In New Orleans cooking, there's the holy trinity that every dish typically begins with: onions, green peppers, and celery. They are similar to the primary colors in that you use them as a foundation to form a thousand variations and make every other color. These same principles are applied to cooking 'cue. Except our triumvirate is formed with heat, smoke, and wood. As long as you have those three essentials, you can achieve your goals in many different ways. Let's break down those bare necessities.

BRINGIN' THE HEAT WITH A GRILL

First, you need a cooking vessel—a grill, smoker, or even an oven—to serve as your heat source. We have recipes written for all three, and you can feel free to vary any of them to fit whatever device you're using. And don't assume you need to buy some fancy, newfangled, chromed-out monster of a grill to be able to smoke, or a smoker designed especially for the task. You can smoke meat on any grill. If you don't have a grill (or a backyard), don't fret. You can still barbecue via a lovely device called the stovetop smoker (though this should be regarded as a last resort, as you could be booted from your dwelling after your neighbors mistake the smoke for an actual fire), which we'll touch on shortly.

As far as outdoor grills go, the main debate always boils down to the source of the heat: charcoal versus gas. Either will get the job done, though we think charcoal tastes better. With charcoal, assuming you're using all-natural briquettes or charwood, which is a natural lump or chunk hardwood, you're cooking on a natural source—wood—which doesn't add any funky flavors to what's sizzling above the briquettes. Gas sometimes does impart a taste to your meat, so if you can avoid it, we suggest you do. That said, if you've already got a propane number in the yard, it will work for the recipes in this book.

One key to the outside grill is the cover. The cover represents a method of control when you're smoking; you have no power over the temperature or how much smoke is enveloping the meat if it's all shooting directly up into the sky. So make sure you've got a solid way to shelter your meats. Vents built into the cover are always a bonus because they afford you the ability to more precisely ensure temperature and smoke volume, but they're not mandatory.

So you've got your charcoal grill, your cover is at the ready, and you're holding a platter of ribs stacked to the sun, chomping at the bit to get 'em laid out atop a crackling fire. Which typically means you'll grab the bottle of lighter fluid, drown the entire bed of charcoal, and toss a match in, cowering and slightly grinning as the whoosh of flames reach higher than your house's roof. But hold off on nearly singeing your eyebrows; lighter fluid—or even the type of charcoal that has lighter fluid embedded—can add an odd taste to the meat, so we recommend keeping the process as pure as possible. You may not get a column of fire shooting up from your grill that's visible from space, but you will end up with more delicious meat.

BRINGIN' THE HEAT WITH A SMOKER

If you don't already have a grill and want to go the smoker route, you can pick one up (for outdoor use) for under $300. Then you can set up this spaceship-looking device in your yard and say things to friends like, "She'll handle a whole pig in about four hours," while they stare on enviously. Simply follow the instructions to operate the individual smoker that you have, and you're all set.

Today we use a variety of types of smokers for a host of purposes. There are gas, electric, wood, and barrel smokers—all of which are equally effective and produce a quality product. Technically, you could dig a sizeable hole, throw some burning charcoal embers in there with some wood and a pork butt, cover the whole thing, and dig it up two days later for a delicious smoked meal, but then you'd have to remember where you put the damn hole, and if you've been drinking, that can be hard. So just stick to the prefabricated smokers for your outdoor needs.

BRINGIN' THE HEAT INSIDE THE HOUSE

For urban apartment dwellers, it's possible to bring the barbecue indoors with a stovetop smoker. It's the easiest way to become known around your building as "the apartment that always smells delicious." These handy devices are about as big as a large aluminum pan and similarly constructed. Camerons makes a solid one that retails for less than $50. Again, this isn't an ideal method, but it will work.

In a stovetop smoker, you can slowly tenderize a small piece of brisket, steaks, or half chickens, or you can even make bacon, but if you want to go bigger—with a pork butt or full piece of brisket—do away with the issued lid and opt for some aluminum foil to cover your dinner. And everything you'll need—including the wood chips—comes with the kit. One quick thing to bear in mind is that none of our recipes are written for a stovetop smoker, so you'll have to be handy

HICKORY is a very hard, dense wood, and one of the most popular used for smoking. It supplies a strong, baconlike flavor that complements meats, leaving a unique aftertaste. Because of its robust flavor, hickory can be mixed with oak for a milder, less overpowering taste. Hickory is often associated with the "classic" American barbecue.

- -

APPLEWOOD smoke supplies a milder, sweeter flavor that is commonly used with pork or poultry.

- -

CHERRY WOOD is similar to apple in taste, leaving a mild, sweet, and fruity flavor. Cherry tends to be a good choice for poultry, fish, or ham. Cherry also gives meat an appealing mahogany color.

- -

OAK is a common favorite in Texas, where it's called post oak. It has a heavy, smoky flavor stronger than apple and cherry, but not as strong as hickory. In general, its smoky taste works best with beef or lamb.

with the modifications to the recipe. Be ready to alter the cooking times and even tend to the smoking a little more than you would in a large device. You'll also have to check the temperature of the meat more often than with an outside unit. We recommend putting an oven thermometer inside to give you a good idea of what temperature your indoor smoker is achieving.

GOT WOOD?

When it comes to barbecue, it's all about slow and low—ask any pit master across the country. The wood you use is a complete matter of personal taste, however. We happen to smoke with hickory and applewood, but at your disposal are the following wood types:

As for the difference between wood chips and wood chunks, we're fans of the chunks. They burn longer in a charcoal grill, you'll use less of them, and, thus, they're the most economical. If you can't find chunks, wood chips will do in a pinch, and for devices like the stovetop smoker, they're the only thing that will likely fit, given the cozy space of the device. You can also use logs, which are very common in industrial smokers or any bigger device. These work best with gas or wood-fueled smokers.

You'll want to soak the wood in water first, to slow down the burning process. Chips should get a bath for an hour, while chunks can go longer, up to overnight. Then—with

GRILLING & SMOKING CHECKLIST

Grilling and smoking are a lot like following any recipe; there is a list of prep work that when followed will ensure perfect food—'cause that's what it's all about, right?

Here's our checklist, modified a bit for the needs of backyard 'cuing.

❏ **KEEP YOUR GRILL GRATES CLEAN.**
Grill grates should be cleaned using a metal bristle grill brush once the grill is preheated and immediately after cooking, while the grill is still hot. (Tip: If your brush comes with a straight metal edge, use that to remove the biggest pieces of food, and follow with the brush.)

❏ **OIL YOUR GRILL GRATES.**
Just before putting food on the preheated grill, the grates should be oiled. This helps keep food from sticking to the grates. To do this, dampen a paper towel with oil and, holding the paper towel with a pair of tongs, rub the paper towel on the grates. Do this quickly, so the paper towel doesn't catch on fire.

❏ **USE A CHIMNEY STARTER.**
This tool, although not required for 'cuing, is very helpful. It allows you to more quickly and evenly light charcoal and to have a preheated portion at the ready when additional fuel is needed during longer barbecuing times. (Adding unlit coals may lower the temperature of the grill and will take longer to catch fire than in a chimney starter. In the worst-case scenario, adding unlit coals to your grill could extinguish the fire.) To use a chimney starter, simply add charcoal in the top, place a crumpled sheet of newspaper or a couple of paraffin or sawdust starters in the bottom of the cylinder, and light the newspaper or starters with a match.

chips—you'll seal them in an aluminum foil pouch. Poke some holes in the pouch and set it on top of the heat source and wait for the first wisps to emerge. With chunks, you'll want to lay them right on the red-hot coals. Sometimes we specify wood chips for foods that are quick-cooking, such as grilled shrimp (typically 1 cup, depending on the size of your chips). In these recipes, using the longer-burning wood chunks would be a waste.

SMOKIN' REMINDER #1:

Remember to presoak wood chunks or chips, following the instructions outlined in "Got Wood?" on page 13.

SMOKIN' REMINDER #2:

Set up your grill for indirect heat. Barbecued foods, typically large chunks of meat, like a brisket, pork shoulder, or an entire pig, are cooked with indirect heat. Direct heat would burn the outside of such large pieces of meat before the inside was fully cooked.

To set up your charcoal grill for cooking with indirect heat, place all your charcoal briquettes on one side of the grill and put a drip pan on the other side. During long, slow cooking, water is added to the pan to help keep the meat moist. The meat goes above the drip pan, and the food is cooked with the lid closed. (The lid directs the smoke in a natural, circular pattern within the chamber, creating an even smoky flavor.)

To set up your gas grill for indirect heat, you'll turn on only half the burners. Put the meat on the side that's cold, where the heat will always be off. You can also place your drip pan below the meat in a gas grill.

If your gas grill doesn't allow you to turn off or lower the heat on one side of your grill, you will not be able to make the low-and-slow barbecued recipes in this book, but there are plenty of direct heat grilling recipes you'll be able to enjoy.

If you have a smoker, you're golden because it's intended for indirect heat. Simply follow the directions that come with it.

SMOKIN' REMINDER #3:

Use a drip pan. When placed beneath meat, it catches grease and reduces flare-ups. During longer barbecuing times, fill the pan with water to help keep the meat moist.

THE FLAVOR ARSENAL

The term *barbecue* has lost some meaning over the years and become synonymous— for most people—with the act of cooking anything on a grill. Any connoisseur of the craft would tell you to take it a step further— that it represents food slowly cooked on a grill, or in a smoker, until it's fork-tender and has assumed a smoky flavor from the smoldering wood. Even if you use unseasoned meat in barbecue, the result is still inherently succulent and tasty.

However, this process of cooking is merely a solid foundation for the endless amount of flavor profiles you can create before the meat hits the grill. The taste of any food is broken down into five categories: sweet, sour, bitter, salty, and savory. With the use of rubs (dry or wet), brines, marinades, basting sauces or mops, and glazes, you can heighten these basic flavor profiles in your barbecued foods, creating a contrast of flavors that will make your taste buds dance.

DRY RUBS, the flavor cornerstone of barbecue, are combinations of dry seasoning, spices, and sometimes dried herbs rubbed onto food before it is cooked. The foundation of nearly every rub is salt, sugar, and pepper, to which a variety of spices may be added. We talk more about dry rubs, including how to make your own, in Chapter 1.

WET RUBS are a combination of spices and herbs that are bound together with liquid or fat, usually oil. Wet rubs may include fresh aromatics, such as garlic or ginger, fresh herbs, and/or dried herbs. Like dry rubs, wet rubs should be massaged into the food, but go easy on delicate foods like fish. Because most wet rubs contain oil, they are useful for keeping lean meats moist during cooking.

BRINES are solutions of salt and sugar dissolved in water, often with flavors added. They're used to pickle vegetables (see Chapter 2), or to tenderize and flavor meats. Brining is particularly popular for poultry. (Tip: Brined foods tend to cook more quickly, so be careful not to overcook.)

MARINADES are liquid combinations, usually comprised of oil, an acid, and flavorings, that bathe foods prior to cooking. They infuse food with flavor, and the acids in them help to soften tissue, making the food more tender. But it's a fine line; foods marinated too long can become mushy. Sometimes marinades serve double duty as basting sauce during grilling. If repurposing a marinade, always make sure to boil it for a few minutes in a nonreactive saucepan before applying it to cooked foods.

BASTING SAUCES/MOPS are liquid mixtures that are applied to food during cooking to keep the food from drying out and to add flavor. These terms are often used interchangeably, though a basting sauce may be bit thicker than a mop (also called a sop). If you want to look really pro, you can pick up a basting mop (a basting tool that looks exactly like a cleaning mop, but in miniature) to apply your mop.

GLAZES are sugary liquids that are brushed on food close to the end of grilling or after the food has been removed from the grill. If applied earlier, the high sugar content would cause the food to burn.

THE TOOL ARSENAL

You don't have to have a restaurant-quality kitchen to replicate the same delicious eats we're plating each day at our Brother Jimmy's locations. In fact, you'd be surprised at how basic the equipment requirements are for barbecue. Remember that this is a simple science; less is often more.

Here are some of basic tools you'll want to have on hand when you're 'cuing:

A METAL SPATULA WITH A LONG HANDLE. You'll want something that won't melt if it should hit the grill by accident.

TONGS. The longer the better, so the flickering flames don't accidentally sear your hand when you're flipping.

HEATPROOF GLOVES. Heavy-duty are always best. Your hands will thank you when handling hot utensils.

A MEAT THERMOMETER. The method of cooking and the time will be determined by your heat source, but internal temperature will always dictate when the food is done. Opt for a thermometer with a probe you can leave in the meat while the readout stays a safe distance away.

AN OVEN THERMOMETER. Use this to sort out the temperature of the grill itself. Built-in thermometers can often be wonky and are not always to be trusted.

HEAVY-DUTY ALUMINUM FOIL. Consider foil the most versatile tool in the barbecue shed. You'll use it more than you'd realize.

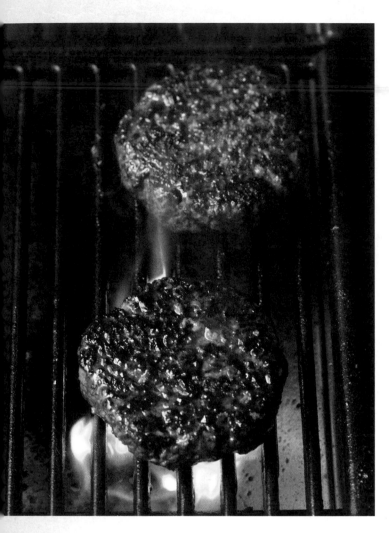

A KITCHEN SYRINGE. This is not an everyday barbecue tool, but is highly useful when you want to inject flavors into your food. We use one to inject Cajun flavors into our Deep-Fried Cajun Chicken (page 172).

A WIRE CLEANING BRUSH. Use this to keep your grill clean. A clean grill is a happy grill.

A COAL RAKE, SMALL FIREPLACE POKER, OR SHOVEL. If you plan to do a lot of 'cuing, rather than straight up direct-heat grilling, you will want something to move hot coals around in your grill or smoker.

A NONREACTIVE PAN. It's important to use pans made of nonreactive material, such as stainless steel or enameled cast iron, when cooking acidic foods like marinades and pickling brines. Otherwise, the reactive metal may impart a metallic taste to your food and can discolor light-colored foods. Reactive metals include aluminum, copper, and cast iron.

A SPICE GRINDER. Use this to freshly grind spices you'll need for the 'cue. You can toast your whole spices, then grind them for a fresher, deeper flavor than what's sitting on your supermarket shelf. If you can't find a spice grinder, a coffee mill doubles nicely.

A MICROPLANE GRATER. We use this to zest citrus and to grate garlic and ginger, among other foods. It creates a really finely grated pile that is perfect for a number of our recipes.

ZIP-TOP BAGS. Great for holding marinated meats. So long as your instruments aren't hot, they can also double as a coaster for your utensils.

A WATER BOTTLE. Shoot it on the grill to cool everything down if the flames get too hot. (Or at friends who try to grab anything off the grill while it's still cooking.)

A BASTING BRUSH. Make sure the bristles are silicone so they won't melt when you're dabbing on the sauce.

A DRIP PAN. Catch all the juice falling from the meat because flame-ups are bad; they burn the meat. You can also add water to the drip pan, which in turn adds moisture to the whole process, producing juicier meat.

POINTERS FROM THE PIG

Throughout this book, we're going to share key barbecue tips with you, plus plenty of great entertaining ideas, brought to you by our porcine pit pal and de facto mascot, Reginald Hammington—a professional party advisor if ever there was one. Good ole Reggie will pop up from time to time to share his vast knowledge with you, so look for his cheery snout in the coming pages.

'CUE BASICS

Hey there. Reggie here. Ready to do this? I've got some basic rules of serving great barbecue for you, because what's the point of slaving the day away cooking if it all falls apart right before you serve it?

LET MEAT REST BEFORE CARVING OR PULLING. I know you'll be anxious to present

---

DEEP-FRYING ESSENTIALS

SINCE WE'RE TALKING ABOUT CRUCIAL TOOLS you'll need handy in the kitchen, it's a good time to break down what you'll need for frying—a process often associated with Southern fare. We recommend you have the following items on hand before you step in front of a vat of bubbling oil.

DEEP-FRYER. This is ideal for frying anything small, like appetizers, popcorn shrimp, or okra, and so forth. It's a self-contained unit with a basket, and you can find them at Kmart or Walmart. Try to resist the urge to deep-fry everything in your fridge and freezer.

DEEP-SIDED POT. If you need to go bigger, you'll want a 5- or 6-quart pot with a heavy bottom. Make sure it's a sturdy level pot that won't tip or shake; many pots end up rocking on the stove, and you can't have that happening with deep-frying.

STRAIGHT-SIDED FRYING PAN. As opposed to regular sauté pans, this one has completely vertical walls, which'll help keep the jumping oil inside. Stainless steel or cast iron works best. Frying pans are used for pan-frying foods that are sitting in a fair amount of oil but not completely submerged as when deep-frying.

TONGS. Tongs supply you with the ability to move, rotate, and turn your food for optimal heat dispersion without burning your hand. The longer

the better. These are also fantastic for pinching unwelcome people who enter your kitchen and try to steal bites before you've plated.

DEEP-FRY THERMOMETER. The temperature of the oil can vary from batch to batch of food, so check it often.

STEEL-WIRE BASKET. Used for deep-frying, this allows the oils to wash over the food, cooking every nook and cranny for a crispy look and taste. Plus, they help you grab entire batches of golden brown heaven all at once.

SLOTTED SPOON OR WIRE MESH SPIDER. If you don't have a wire basket, you'll need one of these to lift the food out of the fryer.

MANDOLINE. This utensil slices vegetables in even slices or crinkled cuts, ideal for tossing into your fryer and great for presentation. Be sure to use the included guard to avoid shaving your knuckles off—the blade is super sharp.

SPLATTER SCREEN. While still allowing air to circulate, the screen will prevent the boiling oil from hitting you in the face or staining your shirt.

DRAIN BOARD OR COOLING RACK. You'll want to line a board with some paper towels, place it in a sheet tray or over a sink, and slant it slightly so that the excess oil has a place to run off the food. Or you can set up a cooling rack over a sheet pan and let the food drain through to the rack.

the proud piece of meat you've labored over as soon as it leaves the grill, but hold on. Always allow pieces to rest before digging into them. The time needed for resting varies based on the size and cut of the meat—beef should rest the longest. This allows juices to redistribute throughout the meat. And everyone will appreciate that when it hits the table.

ALWAYS CUT MEAT ACROSS THE GRAIN. This is a good rule of thumb to follow, but is especially imperative when slicing cuts of meat coming from the chest, shoulders, and legs—generally anything the animal used for walking around. Naturally, those cuts of meat will have more muscle fibers, which can make for chewy, fibrous meat if not sliced properly. This doesn't happen with pork as much as it does steak—that's because pigs are better than cows, but I'm getting off topic. To cut meat across the grain, identify the fibers in the meat. They will all be running in the same direction. Lay the piece of meat in front of you, with the fibers running from left to right. Then cut perpendicular to the fibers, or "across the grain," as they say. Cuts that will have particularly pronounced fibers include flank steak, hanger steak, skirt steak, brisket, and London broil.

WHEN SAUCING BARBECUED MEATS, DON'T OVERDO IT. The point of barbecue is to taste the meat. After all, if you've made our Carolina-Style Pulled Pork (page 118) or Smoked Brisket (page 139), you will have spent hours, not minutes, to achieve deeply flavored, wonderfully smoky, and tender meat. Why cover up your work with too much barbecue sauce?

BRING ON THE FUN

I'll be back shortly with some more tips on the grub, but you'll also see me breaking down the lighter side of any festivity. That includes:

GAMES, GAMES, AND MORE GAMES. Whether you're planning a Final Four party, Super Bowl blowout, a St. Patty's Day bash, or an old-fashioned backyard barbecue, we have lots of games to keep your guests amused. And to help them to put down a few more drinks because a number of the games are liquor-centric.

PLAYLISTS. Music is the backbone of any party. It sets the mood and the tempo and dictates the dancing. Our Essential Playlist (opposite) is a no-fail energizer, and it's suitable for any party. In addition, you'll find other playlists sprinkled throughout the book, crafted with specific themes in mind—like tailgating, a Southern-style "boil" party, Final Four, and more. (If you're going to DJ a pig pickin', do me a little favor and play "Taps" for my fallen brethren? It's only right.)

DRINKS. We keep things simple at Brother Jimmy's. Besides great food, great music, and fun games, there's only one other crucial element necessary to throwing a memorable party: drinks. Although, depending on how many drinks you have, the memories may be hazy. In addition to giving you recipes for our most popular drinks, I'll share my favorite drinking tips with you—like how much of the silly sauce to have on hand, how to chill beer like a pro, and what to serve your drinks in.

ESSENTIAL PLAYLIST

Just as many of our recipes are classic dishes, these songs are classic Brother Jimmy's. You'll hear them anytime you go to any of our restaurants. They're the perfect songs to go along with any party, event, or meal. Always have 'em handy.

TIM McGRAW
SOMETHING LIKE THAT
(BBQ STAIN)

ALAN JACKSON
IT'S FIVE O'CLOCK SOMEWHERE

DIERKS BENTLEY
HOW AM I DOIN'

JOHN COUGAR MELLENCAMP
SMALL TOWN

O.A.R.
THAT WAS A CRAZY GAME
OF POKER

TOM PETTY
AMERICAN GIRL

LYNYRD SKYNYRD
SWEET HOME ALABAMA

LENNY KRAVITZ
AMERICAN WOMAN

BRUCE SPRINGSTEEN
GLORY DAYS

JIMMY BUFFETT
CHANGES IN LATITUDES,
CHANGES IN ATTITUDES

ALABAMA
SONG OF THE SOUTH

DIXIE CHICKS
GOODBYE EARL

GARTH BROOKS
AMERICAN HONKY-TONK
BAR ASSOCIATION

TOBY KEITH
WHISKEY GIRL

CREEDENCE CLEARWATER REVIVAL
DOWN ON THE CORNER

THE CHARLIE DANIELS BAND
THE DEVIL WENT DOWN
TO GEORGIA

AC/DC
HAVE A DRINK ON ME

VAN HALEN
RUNNIN' WITH THE DEVIL

BON JOVI
LIVIN' ON A PRAYER

EDDIE MONEY
TAKE ME HOME TONIGHT

THE ROLLING STONES
GIMME SHELTER

U2
NEW YEAR'S DAY

CHAPTER Nº 1

CORE RUBS, SPICES & SAUCES

RUBS WERE ORIGINALLY
APPLIED OUT OF NECESSITY, NOT FOR FLAVOR.

Developed in the days before refrigeration, heaps of salt and sugar were rubbed on cuts of meat to help preserve the slab for as long as possible. When the meat was cooked, there was an unexpected and delicious by-product—it was bursting with flavor. In the centuries since, the rub has come to define the flavor of any barbecue, as they're now a matter of personal preference, geographical region, and taste. Although any barbecue aficionado will tell you that the meat itself makes for great barbecue, they all acknowledge that the rub adds your signature flavor and personality to the meat.

The basic rub often, but not always, includes salt, sugar, ground black pepper, and spices, such as cumin, paprika, chili powder, granulated garlic, and granulated onion (garlic and onion powders taste too medicinal). The spices are dubbed "transitional" spices because they help smooth out, fill in, and add dimension to what would otherwise be a sharply contrasting set of flavors if only sweet, salty, and peppery notes were used.

Sugar is great because it adds another layer of taste, igniting fireworks in your mouth and on your tongue. Rubs vary for the type of meat, particularly between pork and beef. For the best flavor, you'll want more sugar on pork than on beef. When you add the salt and other spices, it's even more action for your taste buds to savor because you're hitting all various palate sensations.

For example, we introduced our Brother Jimmy's Southern Rub about four years ago, based on a Memphis-style dry rub. It's sweeter than our Brother Jimmy's Dry Rub thanks to dark brown sugar, yet it's still got some kick from the ancho chile powder and ground yellow mustard. For our pulled pork, the pork butt we're smoking is encased in the signature Brother Jimmy's Dry Rub, which uses seasoned salt as a base and is heightened by about twenty dried spices, including fennel seed and rosemary. The resulting flavor profile ends up being close to sausage, in part owing to the fennel seed, a very unique approach to the dry rub.

The cool thing about rubs, and barbecue in general, is that although there is a fundamental set of constants, how you adapt a recipe within your kitchen is entirely up to you. We're here to give you our take and methods, but you can do whatever makes you happy. Southern cooking is often about family recipes, passed down on note cards in weathered boxes over the generations.

Everyone has his or her unique take on a particular Southern staple and no one recipe is ever better or worse. It's all about personal preference, so you should get as creative as you'd like.

This chapter will highlight core rubs that we're dredging our cuts of meat in at each Brother Jimmy's location. Feel free to whip them up as outlined or to get innovative. The rub creation process is entirely a trial-and-error one. Simply start with a solid base of salt, sugar, and black pepper, and pick some flavors you like, such as chili powder or paprika, adding them teaspoon by teaspoon to create the final flavor you want. If you overdo one spice, cut it down by adding more base. Taste it while dry after each addition, but be sure to write down what you're doing step-by-step for future use.

We'll also go over sauces, because what's better than tangy sauce running down the sides of a pile of steaming barbecue? Topping our restaurants' tables are five squirt bottles, each containing a different trademark sauce. The differences between the drips are vast because Southern barbecue sauces vary by region; just a few ingredients can set similar recipes apart by miles when it comes to consistency and taste. Because Brother Jimmy's roots lie in North Carolina, the predominant sauce is our Eastern Carolina Sauce, which serves as a base for our Original BBQ, Chipotle BBQ, and Blazin' sauces. In addition, we also have a Mustard BBQ Sauce, which is a key component to South Carolina barbecue.

THE COOL THING ABOUT RUBS,
AND BARBECUE IN GENERAL,
is that while there is a fundamental set of constants, how you adapt a recipe within your kitchen is entirely up to you.

Our Eastern Carolina Sauce follows tradition in that it's thinner and based on a mix of vinegar and crushed red pepper flakes. It pairs astoundingly well with pulled pork and doubles as an ingredient for a spicy vinaigrette, perfect for making coleslaw with a smidgen of a kick (page 49). Historically, Eastern Carolina settlers believed that the tomato was poisonous, so they didn't include the fruit into the mix. But Western Carolinians weren't afraid of the little red guys, so their version includes them as well as a pile of brown sugar for a sweeter taste, as both soften the vinegar. Brother Jimmy's Original BBQ Sauce is our take on the Western Carolina–based sauce.

From these two staples, simple variations to the recipes form the other sauces. Blazin' sears your tongue with the addition of cayenne pepper, and pureed chipotle heats up the Chipotle BBQ Sauce. However you choose to top your 'cue, we've got a sauce recipe for you. The important thing to remember is that barbecue is about the meat. The lighter you can make your drips, the happier you'll be, because you don't want to drown out the flavors of the protein you just cooked.

(By the way, if you're looking for premade sauces and rubs to speed up your prep time, we can help you out in that department. We sell four of our five key barbecue sauces—plus our original dry rub—in our restaurants and on our website. We're always developing and honing new flavors, so because good books, like good barbecue, take a while to make, be sure to check our locations and website for the latest offerings.)

BROTHER JIMMY'S
DRY RUB

This is our original signature dry rub that's been gracing our plates since 1989. We dare you to find another one like it.

1 In a mortar and pestle or in a spice grinder, coarsely crush the rosemary, taking care not to grind it into a powder.

2 Repeat Step 1 with the fennel seeds.

3 Combine all the ingredients in a small bowl and store in an airtight container.

- 2 tablespoons dried rosemary
- ¼ cup fennel seeds
- ¾ cup Lawry's Seasoned Salt
- 2¾ teaspoons granulated garlic
- 5 teaspoons cayenne pepper
- 1½ tablespoons dried thyme
- ¼ cup crushed red pepper flakes
- 2 tablespoons ground dried sage
- ¼ cup dried basil
- ½ cup dried mint
- 2¼ teaspoons ground white pepper
- 4½ teaspoons ground black pepper

MAKES about 2½ cups (more than enough for 3 racks)

25 ★ CORE RUBS, SPICES & SAUCES

BROTHER JIMMY'S
SOUTHERN RUB

¼ cup brown sugar

¼ cup kosher salt

2 tablespoons paprika

1 tablespoon ground black pepper

1 tablespoon ancho chile powder

1½ teaspoons dry mustard

1 teaspoon granulated garlic

1 teaspoon granulated onion

MAKES about ¾ cup (enough for 3 racks)

It's our Memphis-style rub, with sugar and spice and everything nice.

Combine all the ingredients in a small bowl and store in an airtight container.

SPICY
FISH RUB

¾ teaspoon cayenne pepper

1½ tablespoons smoked paprika

4½ tablespoons chili powder

1½ tablespoons ground cumin

1½ tablespoons ground coriander

1½ tablespoons ground black pepper

1½ tablespoons kosher salt

MAKES about ¾ cup

We created this spicy rub for catfish, but it'll work well with any mild to medium-flavored fish. If you like sweet and spice together, try the Sweet and Spicy Catfish (page 199). There we combine this rub with brown sugar and butter for maximum flavor.

Combine the ingredients in a small bowl and store in an airtight container.

EASTERN CAROLINA
BBQ SAUCE

BRISKET SUGAR SHAKE

BROTHER JIMMY'S
DRY RUB

BROTHER JIMMY'S
MUSTARD BBQ SAUCE

BROTHER JIMMY'S
ORIGINAL BBQ SAUCE

BROTHER JIMMY'S
SOUTHERN RUB

FRESH HERB AND GARLIC
RUB

¼ cup fresh parsley

¼ cup fresh oregano

1 tablespoon fresh thyme

4 garlic cloves

1 tablespoon kosher salt

½ teaspoon ground black pepper

6 tablespoons olive oil

MAKES about ¾ cup

This wet rub goes nicely with sirloin steak (page 151), but any cut of steak will be happy to have this topping it. You can even try it with chicken or pork or a particularly meaty piece of fish, such as salmon or tuna.

1 Chop the herbs, then combine them in a medium bowl.

2 Place the garlic on a cutting board and smash it with the side of a large chef's knife. Place the salt on top of the smashed garlic and begin chopping together. Using the side of your knife, spread the garlic and salt around to smash them together. Continue smashing and chopping until you have a paste. (Salt acts as an abrasive, helping to grind the garlic to a smooth paste.)

3 Add the garlic-salt paste to the herbs and mix in the pepper and oil. Use immediately or store in a covered container in the refrigerator for up to 3 days.

BRISKET
SUGAR SHAKE

½ cup turbinado sugar

4½ tablespoons "brownulated" light brown sugar

4½ teaspoons kosher salt

¾ teaspoon ground black pepper

MAKES just over 1 cup

Once your brisket is sliced on the plate, give it a little sprinkle with this shake to round out the rich, fatty flavor of the beef.

Combine all the ingredients in a small bowl and store in an airtight container.

BLACKENING SPICE

A traditional spice mix that adds a delicious smoky and spicy flavor to foods, this was originally developed for fish but has been adapted well for pork, shrimp, and even vegetables. This is our version of the Cajun classic.

Combine all the ingredients in a small bowl and store in an airtight container.

- ½ cup chili powder
- ¾ teaspoon dried thyme
- ¾ teaspoon dried basil
- ¾ teaspoon dried oregano
- ¾ teaspoon granulated onion
- ¾ teaspoon granulated garlic
- ¼ teaspoon ground black pepper
- ¼ teaspoon ground white pepper
- ¼ teaspoon kosher salt
- ⅛ teaspoon cayenne pepper

MAKES just over ½ cup

EASTERN CAROLINA BBQ SAUCE

This is the classic eastern North Carolina sauce, which doesn't include tomato. The combination of this and pork butt create the staple Carolina Pulled Pork—our quintessential dish.

Combine all the ingredients in a lidded container and shake well. Use immediately or store for later use in the refrigerator, where it will keep for months. Shake well before using.

- 1½ cups white vinegar
- ½ cup water
- 1½ teaspoons cayenne pepper
- 1½ teaspoons crushed red pepper flakes
- 1½ teaspoons dark brown sugar
- ¾ teaspoon table salt

MAKES about 2 cups

BOURBON
BBQ SAUCE

2 tablespoons olive oil

½ cup minced Spanish onion

2 tablespoons minced garlic

1 teaspoon ground allspice

½ teaspoon ground ginger

¼ teaspoon dry mustard

¼ teaspoon ground coriander

¼ teaspoon ground cumin

2 tablespoons light
brown sugar

3 tablespoons soy sauce

2 tablespoons Frank's Red
Hot Sauce

2 tablespoons Worcestershire
sauce

2 tablespoons red wine vinegar

1⅛ cups tomato paste

1 cup molasses

1¾ cups water

6 tablespoons good bourbon

MAKES 4 cups

This recipe makes a fair amount of sauce, which is a good thing, as it's great on pork and chicken as well as Smoked Brisket (page 139). When catering, we even put it on smoked tofu. It'll keep for several months in the fridge, and it's just as tasty cold, pulled right out of the fridge.

1 Heat the oil in a medium saucepan over medium heat. Add the onion and garlic and sauté until softened, about 5 minutes.

2 Add the spices and brown sugar and mix well. Add the soy sauce, hot sauce, Worcestershire sauce, and vinegar.

3 Add the tomato paste and stir to break it all up and incorporate it, then stir in the molasses.

4 Slowly add the water to make a smooth sauce, then add the bourbon and simmer for 30 minutes. Cool and store in the refrigerator in a glass jar with a tight-fitting lid.

BROTHER JIMMY'S ORIGINAL BBQ SAUCE

This is our core sauce based on the western North Carolina style. It's a good idea to keep extra in the fridge because it goes well with everything from fries to chicken fingers.

1 Whisk all the ingredients together in a nonreactive saucepan, place over medium-high heat, and bring to a boil.

2 Lower the heat and simmer for 15 to 20 minutes, until the sauce just coats the back of a wooden spoon—it's not intended to be overly thick.

3 Cool and use immediately or store for later use in the fridge, where it will keep for 2 to 3 months.

2 cups white vinegar

1½ cups Heinz ketchup (if you use another brand, the taste will be different)

1½ cups packed dark brown sugar

2 tablespoons chili powder

1½ teaspoons ground black pepper

1 tablespoon kosher salt

MAKES about 5 cups

BLAZIN' SAUCE

Cayenne pepper gives our Original BBQ Sauce an infusion of heat in this spicy sauce. For those of you who like things hot, a bottle of this will be your best friend.

1 recipe Brother Jimmy's Original BBQ Sauce (above)

6½ tablespoons cayenne pepper

MAKES about 5 cups

Follow the Original BBQ Sauce recipe, adding the cayenne with the other ingredients.

CHIPOTLE PUREE

1 (7-ounce) can chipotles in adobo sauce

MAKES ½ cup

Chipotle Puree is a staple in our kitchens. It adds a little heat and a subtle smoke flavor to many of our dishes—in fact, it's great in just about anything (even chocolate cake!).

1 Place a mesh strainer over a bowl. Empty the can of chipotles into the strainer. We recommend wearing rubber gloves while handling the chipotles, and remember not to touch your face. It will burn.

2 Remove the seeds from the chiles while reserving the chiles and the liquid that has drained into the bowl.

3 Once the seeds are removed, transfer the liquid and chiles to a blender and blend until you have a smooth puree. Store the puree in the refrigerator in a glass jar, where it will keep for a few months.

GUAVA
BBQ SAUCE

1 tablespoon tomato paste

¼ cup red wine vinegar

¼ cup light brown sugar

1 cup diced Spanish onion

¼ cup garlic cloves, smashed after measuring

2 cups water

1 tablespoon dark chili powder

2 tablespoons fresh lime juice

8 ounces guava paste, cut up (found in the Latin section of your supermarket)

½ teaspoon kosher salt

MAKES 4 cups

This sauce was made for our Grilled Salmon (page 198), but it also perfectly complements other fatty fish like mahi mahi as well as grilled pork.

1 Combine all the ingredients in a nonreactive saucepan, place over medium heat, and bring to a simmer. Reduce the heat and simmer for 20 to 30 minutes, until the onion and garlic soften.

2 Transfer to a blender and blend until smooth—be careful that hot liquid doesn't spurt out. Use immediately or cool to room temperature and store in an airtight container in the refrigerator for up to 4 weeks.

BROTHER JIMMY'S
MUSTARD BBQ SAUCE

Mustard sauce is what really differentiates South Carolina pulled pork from its Northern cousin. This sauce is also great with veggies and grilled shrimp.

1 Whisk together all the ingredients in a medium nonreactive saucepan.

2 Place over medium-high heat and bring to a boil, stirring often, then turn off the heat.

3 Use immediately or let cool and store in an airtight container in the refrigerator for up to 4 weeks.

1 cup cider vinegar

1 cup yellow mustard, such as French's

3 tablespoons dark brown sugar

Heaping ¼ teaspoon ground black pepper

⅛ teaspoon cayenne pepper

4½ teaspoons chili powder

1 teaspoon Frank's Red Hot Sauce

2¼ teaspoons soy sauce

MAKES about 2¼ cups

BROTHER JIMMY'S
CHIPOTLE
BBQ SAUCE

This recipe takes our Original BBQ Sauce and ratchets it up a notch with a little smoke and heat from our spicy friend the chipotle. We use it on our smoked and grilled wings and our BBQ Burger, among other dishes.

¼ cup Chipotle Puree (page 32)

4 cups Brother Jimmy's Original BBQ Sauce (page 31)

MAKES 4¼ cups

Combine the Chipotle Puree with the BBQ Sauce and whisk until well combined. Use immediately or store in the refrigerator for months in a glass jar with a tightly fitting lid.

CHAPTER № 2

CONDIMENTS, PICKLES & SLAWS

WE'D BE REMISS

IN NOT TALKING ABOUT A STAPLE OF ANY BIG BARBECUE

bash: the condiments, pickles, and slaws. It's typical Southern tradition to have this trio on hand, and most 'cuing festivities dedicate an entire table to these accoutrements, so it's only fitting that we give them a chapter of their own.

Often in Southern restaurants, your starters are pickles and slaw. A heaping bowl of each usually hits the table as soon as you sit down, keeping diners contented as they nosh on crunchy bites while perusing the menu. Cucumbers steeped in brine or vinegar have adorned plates, burgers, and other dishes since pickling was first invented. These delicious and salty treats are often a standard accompaniment to Southern fare and, when battered and fried, are elevated from being a garnish or side dish to the main plate. (Our version of the latter, Frickles, is on page 76.) And pickles often come out with each dish in our restaurants, because when you're eating heavy barbecue food, there's nothing like a bite of a bright, crisp pickle to refresh your mouth.

Whether you like them whole, sliced, raw, or fried—or soaked in Kool-Aid and dubbed Koolickles, as kids in the South call them—pickles always round out the palate nicely. It doesn't always have to be a cucumber that's getting the pickling treatment. We've got some other favorite brined-and-canned options for you. Simply pick your favorite veggie and get to picklin'.

As for coleslaw, it's not only a creamy side in its own right, but also an integral ingredient in a number of our dishes. It tops our Classic Pulled-Pork sandwich and provides a perfect bed for our Garlic, Jalapeño, and Lime–Brined Chicken. The tanginess of the slaw really complements any number of smoked or grilled meats, and we've got a few slaw recipes for you in the coming pages, including our Rainbow Slaw, our original Creamy Coleslaw, and our Spicy Carolina Slaw, which has a nice kick thanks to the addition of our Eastern Carolina BBQ Sauce.

Finally, there are condiments. Many of ours are multi-use. You can use our Blue Cheese Dressing as a dip for wings, to dress a salad, or to top our Buffalo Chicken Sandwich. We use our Buttermilk Ranch Dressing as a dip for our Chipotle Wings and as the sauce for our Jalapeño Poppers. Our Cajun Mayonnaise is the perfect sauce for our Popcorn Shrimp and is used as a spread on our Catfish Po' Boys. We've got every sauce and dip in the coming pages, so no matter what your favorite condiment is, we've got you covered.

BLUE CHEESE
DRESSING

1 cup Hellman's mayonnaise
½ cup crumbled blue cheese
Pinch of ground white pepper
¾ teaspoon fresh lime juice
1 teaspoon fresh lemon juice
¼ teaspoon kosher salt
4 teaspoons sour cream

MAKES 1¾ cups

We use this dressing to make you want to eat your salad greens, but it also serves as a fantastic dip for just about anything—especially our Buffalo Wings (page 169).

Place all the ingredients in a bowl and whisk well. It'll keep for 2 weeks in the fridge in a container with a tight-fitting lid.

BUFFALO
SAUCE

1½ cups Frank's Red Hot Sauce
2 tablespoons sugar
¾ teaspoon cayenne pepper
¾ teaspoon chili powder
2 tablespoons cold unsalted butter, cut into cubes

MAKES about 2 cups

If you do wing night right, you'll end up wearing some of this, so opt out of donning white. It's great for spicing up anything: Put it on your chicken or in your eggs, or with your home fries or on a hot dog. We use it as a dip for fried okra, too. It's so versatile you'll want to keep a jar on hand at all times.

1 Pour the hot sauce into a small saucepan, place over medium heat, and bring to a boil.

2 In a small bowl, combine the sugar, cayenne, and chili powder. Whisk into the hot sauce, mixing well.

3 Remove the pan from the heat and whisk the butter into the sauce.

4 Use immediately or cover and refrigerate for up to 2 to 3 weeks.

BUTTERMILK
RANCH DRESSING

We pair this with our Jalapeño Poppers (page 84), but it's also great atop a salad or alongside a crudité platter.

In a large bowl, whisk all the ingredients together. It will keep for 1 week in the refrigerator in a container with a tight-fitting lid.

1 cup Hellman's mayonnaise

1¼ cups buttermilk

½ cup sour cream

2 scallions, green parts only, very thinly sliced

¼ teaspoon Frank's Red Hot Sauce

¼ teaspoon granulated onion

¼ teaspoon granulated garlic

¼ teaspoon ground black pepper

¼ teaspoon salt

¼ teaspoon ground white pepper

MAKES 2½ cups

HONEY MUSTARD

This pulls double duty as a dip for fried chicken or a salad dressing with some zing.

In a medium bowl, whisk together all the ingredients. It will keep for 1 month in the refrigerator.

½ cup spicy brown mustard (like Gulden's)

1 cup honey

¼ cup Brother Jimmy's Original BBQ Sauce (page 31)

1 tablespoon Buffalo Sauce (page 36; you can substitute hot sauce if you like)

MAKES 1¾ cups

ROASTED TOMATO
TARTAR
SAUCE

3 oven-roasted plum tomatoes (see Note), cooled and chopped

¾ cup Hellman's mayonnaise

2 tablespoons chopped dill pickle

2 tablespoons finely chopped scallion

1½ teaspoons fresh lemon juice

4½ teaspoons finely chopped red onion

½ teaspoon salt

¼ teaspoon Frank's Red Hot Sauce

Freshly ground black pepper to taste

MAKES about 1½ cups

We use this as the accompanying dip for our Cornmeal-Crusted Catfish Nuggets (page 87) and on our Catfish Po' Boys (page 187), but you can serve it alongside other fish dishes.

Combine all the ingredients in a medium bowl. It will keep for about 1 week in the refrigerator.

NOTE To roast the tomatoes, cut them into quarters and sprinkle them with about ½ teaspoon salt, ¼ teaspoon sugar, and a dash of black pepper. Place on a baking rack over a sheet pan and bake for about 1 hour at 275°F, until they start to dry out a little.

CAJUN MAYONNAISE

We use this as a spread for our Po' Boys (page 187). It also goes well with our Popcorn Shrimp (page 86) and alongside any raw veggies, or you can use it on a sandwich for a tangy kick.

1 large red pepper

1 cup Hellman's mayonnaise

2 teaspoons Blackening Spice (page 29)

¼ teaspoon kosher salt

¾ teaspoon paprika

¼ teaspoon cayenne pepper

1 teaspoon fresh lemon juice

1 teaspoon Worcestershire sauce

¼ teaspoon Frank's Red Hot Sauce

MAKES 1½ cups

1 Roast the red pepper by placing it over an open flame—a hot grill or gas burner on your home stove works well. Turn it frequently until the skin has charred and starts to blister from the flame. Place the pepper in a small bowl and cover with plastic wrap—or you can seal it in an airtight container. Let rest for 10 to 15 minutes. This allows the skin to separate from the meat a little and makes for easier peeling. When the pepper is cool enough to handle, peel off all the charred skin and remove the seeds.

2 Mince the pepper as fine as you can.

3 Place in a medium bowl, add the remaining ingredients, and whisk until the ingredients are well incorporated. Use immediately or store in the refrigerator for up to 1 week.

PICKLED RED ONIONS

¾ cup water

1 cup champagne vinegar

1½ teaspoon kosher salt

2 teaspoons sugar

2 bay leaves

1 teaspoon whole black peppercorns

2 large red onions, sliced into ¼-inch rounds

MAKES 1 pint

These are a "quick" pickle and do not require processing. They will last for a couple of weeks in the refrigerator. We also use the liquid as a seasoning for potato salad. They're the perfect accompaniment to Puerto Rican Mojo Ribs (page 117) or Grilled Chipotle-Orange Pork Loin (page 123).

1 Combine all the ingredients except the onions in a 2-quart nonreactive pot. Place over medium heat, bring to a simmer, and simmer until the salt and sugar dissolve.

2 Remove from the heat and add the onions. Cool completely, then pack into a glass pint jar and refrigerate until ready to use.

PICKLED BELL PEPPERS

PICKLED CHIPTOLE
STRING BEANS

MOM'S BEST SUMMER KIRBIES

PICKLED CAULIFLOWER

PICKLED RED ONIONS

MOM'S BEST
SUMMER
KIRBIES

4 cups cold water

2 tablespoons kosher salt

2 tablespoons pickling spice

5 or 6 garlic cloves

3 to 4 fresh dill sprigs

2 pounds firm Kirby cucumbers without blemishes

MAKES 2 pounds

Make crocks of these with the first of the summer Kirbies, as they're very simple to make. Bear in mind that this is a base recipe, in that we've given you basic proportions for the brine—adjust as you see fit. You will need to buy some cheesecloth for this recipe.

1 In a medium saucepan, combine 1 cup of the water and the salt. Heat the water until the salt dissolves. Add the remaining water, the pickling spice, garlic, and dill.

2 Place the cucumbers in a crock or a large glass jar. Pour the brine over the cucumbers to cover by 1 inch. Lay a triple layer of cheesecloth over the mouth of the jar.

3 Place the jar in a cool, dry place; the pickles will be ready in 2 to 5 days. Be sure to check the pickles after 2 days—if a scum begins to form, carefully pull off the cheesecloth, rinse it out, and place it back on the jar. The pickles will keep for a few weeks in the refrigerator.

PICKLED
BELL PEPPERS

Make sure to vary the colors of peppers you're using for this. The more diverse the selection, the prettier the jars look when you're finished.

1 Cut the peppers into 1-inch strips and set aside with the garlic.

2 Combine the remaining ingredients in a large nonreactive pot, place over medium heat, and bring to a simmer. Simmer until the salt and sugar dissolve.

3 Meanwhile, fill your canning pot with water and bring to a boil.

4 Bring another, smaller pot of water to a simmer. Clean 8 pint jars in hot, soapy water and place the two-part lids in the smaller pot of simmering water until ready to use.

5 Remove the lids from the water and dry with a clean, lint-free cloth.

6 Place 2 cloves of garlic in each pint jar, then fill the jars with the pepper slices.

7 Bring the brine back up to a boil and pour it into the jars, filling each to ¼ inch from the top. Place the lids on and loosely secure.

8 Place the jars into the canning pot and process for 15 minutes. Remove the jars and set aside to cool at room temperature, away from drafts, for several hours. You might hear tiny pops as the jars seal themselves from the pressure. If you have any jars that don't seal (you can tell by pressing the center of the lid—if it moves, it didn't seal), store them in the refrigerator and eat within a couple of weeks. When they have cooled completely, secure the ring band and store in a cool, dry place. Once opened, they'll keep for 1 month in the refrigerator.

5 pounds bell peppers (mixed colors)

16 garlic cloves

3½ cups water

3½ cups white vinegar

¼ cup garlic cloves

1 tablespoon kosher salt

½ cup sugar

½ red onion, cut into quarters

1 tablespoon whole black peppercorns

½ teaspoon mustard seeds

4 whole cloves

3 allspice berries

2 bay leaves

MAKES 8 pints

PICKLED
JALAPEÑOS

12 garlic cloves

6 cups cider vinegar

5 teaspoons kosher salt

1 teaspoon mustard seeds

½ teaspoon whole black peppercorns

2 bay leaves

1 cinnamon stick

4 allspice berries

2 pounds jalapeños

½ pound carrots, thinly sliced

MAKES 6 pints

The mixture of the vinegar with the heat of the jalapeños combines for a flavorful medley in your mouth. You can also use these for the Jalapeño Poppers on page 84.

1   Combine all the ingredients except the jalapeños and carrots in a large nonreactive pot, place over medium heat, and bring to a simmer. Simmer until the salt and sugar dissolve.

2   Meanwhile, get water in your canning pot up to a boil. Clean 6 pint jars in hot, soapy water and place the two-part lids in a pot of simmering water on the stove. Leave them in the water until ready to use.

3   Remove the lids from the water and dry with a clean, lint-free cloth.

4   Divide the jalapeños among the jars and divide the carrot slices on top.

5   Bring the brine back up to a boil and pour it into the jars, filling each to ¼ inch from the top. Place the lids on and loosely secure.

6   Place the jars into the canning pot and process for 12 minutes. Remove the jars from the water bath and set aside to cool at room temperature, away from drafts, for several hours. You might hear tiny pops as the jars seal themselves from the pressure. If you have any jars that don't seal (you can tell by pressing the center of the lid—if it moves, it didn't seal), store them in the refrigerator and eat within a couple of weeks. When they have cooled completely, secure the ring band and store in a cool, dry place.

PICKLED
CHIPOTLE
STRING BEANS

We use these in our Bloody Mary drinks at the restaurants, which make Sunday brunch that much better—but they're perfect for snacking on, too.

1 Place all the ingredients except the string beans in a large nonreactive pot, place over medium heat, and bring to a boil. Reduce the heat and simmer until the salt dissolves.

2 Meanwhile, get the water in your canning pot up to a boil. Clean 8 quart jars in hot, soapy water and place the two-part lids in a pot of simmering water on the stove until ready to use.

3 Remove the lids from the water and dry with a clean, lint-free cloth.

4 Place the string beans in the jars with the pointy ends up.

5 Bring the brine back up to a boil and pour it into the jars, filling each to ¼ inch from the top. Place the lids on and loosely secure.

6 Place the jars into the canning pot and process for 12 minutes. Remove the jars from the water bath and set aside to cool at room temperature, away from drafts, for several hours. You might hear tiny pops as the jars seal themselves from the pressure. If you have any jars that don't seal (you can tell by pressing the center of the lid—if it moves, it didn't seal), store them in the refrigerator and eat within a couple of weeks. When they have cooled completely, secure the ring band and store in a cool, dry place.

2¼ quarts white vinegar

2½ quarts water

1¼ cups kosher salt

3 tablespoons mustard seeds

3 tablespoons celery seeds

2 tablespoons coriander seeds

2 tablespoons chipotle chile powder

½ cup garlic cloves

3 bay leaves

8 to 10 pounds string beans, stem ends trimmed

MAKES 8 quarts

PICKLED
CAULIFLOWER

4 cups cider vinegar

2 cups water

¼ cup sugar

2 tablespoons mustard seeds

2 tablespoons salt

1 teaspoon ground turmeric

3 garlic cloves

2 heads cauliflower, cut into 1-inch florets

8 whole cloves

MAKES 8 pints

Many people find cauliflower bland, which is why it is often drenched with butter and piled high with mounds of cheese. This brine is a simple and low-fat way to get the white vegetable spiced up with a burst of flavor.

1 Combine all the ingredients except the cauliflower and whole cloves in a large nonreactive saucepan, place over medium heat, and bring to a simmer. Simmer until the salt and sugar dissolve.

2 Meanwhile, get the water in your canning pot up to a boil. Clean 8 pint jars in hot, soapy water and place the two-part lids in a pot of simmering water on the stove until ready to use.

3 Remove the lids from the water and dry with a clean, lint-free cloth.

4 Pack the cauliflower into the jars and add 1 whole clove to each.

5 Bring the brine back up to a boil and pour it into the jars, filling each to ¼ inch from the top. Place the lids on and loosely secure.

6 Place the jars into the canning pot and process for 15 minutes. Remove the jars from the water bath and set aside to cool at room temperature, away from drafts, for several hours. You might hear tiny pops as the jars seal themselves from the pressure. If you have any jars that don't seal (you can tell by pressing the center of the lid—if it moves, it didn't seal), store them in the refrigerator and eat within a couple of weeks. When they have cooled completely, secure the ring band and store in a cool, dry place.

CREAMY COLESLAW

This rich coleslaw is great on its own or as a topping for an array of sandwiches, like pulled pork—which is the traditional way it's served in North Carolina. If you want a lighter slaw, try our Rainbow Slaw (page 48) or our Spicy Carolina Slaw (page 49).

½ medium head green cabbage

2 scallions

1 cup Hellman's mayonnaise

4½ tablespoons white vinegar

¼ teaspoon ground thyme

½ teaspoon celery seeds

½ teaspoon kosher salt

½ teaspoon sugar

SERVES 6 to 8

1 Finely shred the cabbage using a box grater or food processor.

2 Thinly slice the green part of the scallion.

3 Whisk together the remaining ingredients in a large bowl. Add the cabbage and scallions and mix until well incorporated. Store in an airtight container in the refrigerator for up to 3 to 4 days.

RAINBOW SLAW

4 cups thinly sliced green cabbage

3 cups thinly sliced red cabbage

1½ cups grated carrots

4 scallions, green parts only, thinly sliced

2 teaspoons salt

½ teaspoon ground black pepper

½ teaspoon ground cumin

2 tablespoons fresh lime juice

1 tablespoon cider vinegar

1 tablespoon olive oil

SERVES 6 to 8

This is the perfect bed for our Garlic, Jalapeño, and Lime–Brined Chicken (page 175), but it also goes great alongside light fish or any other summer treats coming off the grill.

Combine all the ingredients in a large bowl and let sit for 45 minutes while the flavors meld. Serve at room temperature or chilled. Store in an airtight container in the refrigerator for up to 3 to 4 days.

SPICY
CAROLINA
SLAW

The addition of our Eastern Carolina BBQ Sauce helps heat up this lighter version of our creamy coleslaw, and a touch of sugar keeps it from being overpowering. We recommend throwing this atop your pulled pork as an alternative to our creamy slaw.

5 cups green cabbage

1 cup grated carrot

2 scallions, chopped

6 tablespoons Eastern Carolina Sauce (page 29)

¼ cup ketchup

4 teaspoons sugar

1 teaspoon salt

SERVES 6 to 8

1 Shred the cabbage using a box grater or food processor.

2 Place the cabbage and carrot in a large bowl.

3 In a small bowl, whisk together the remaining ingredients. Add to the cabbage and carrot and mix well.

4 Let the slaw sit for at least 30 minutes or up to 24 hours before serving. Store in an airtight container in the refrigerator for up to 4 days.

CHAPTER № 3

DRINKS

WHEN CREATING THE

PERFECT PARTY, DRINKS ARE AN ESSENTIAL COMPONENT.

Brother Jimmy's is, historically, as much a nightspot as it is a restaurant, and the popularity of our specialty drinks is a testament to that fact. The range of drinks we offer covers pretty much everything you'll need or want at any party, be it a Final Four bash or a backyard barbecue.

We've got drinks the ladies will love—like Palmetto Punch, Sangria (two ways), and Frozen Margaritas—many of which are so delicious that the lasses will often ask if there's any booze in there (there is). And we've got some manly drinks that can put hair on your chest—such as the Mint Julep (aka Hair of the Dog), Charlotte Tea, and Louisville Lemonade. We've even got drinks to wake up with, such as our Battle of Antietam Bloody Mary and our Bloody Beer (a beer-based take on the classic brunch cocktail).

Planning to have a big blowout and don't want to mess with individual drinks? We've got recipes for party-size libations, too. We're talking fishbowls and huge punch-bowl cocktails, because isn't everything always a little more festive when the drinks come in gallons? And if you're looking to go from zero to sixty, we've got a fine array of shooters and bombs in store for you. They're always assured to get the party started. Quickly.

Ironically, many of the Southern towns where barbecue reigns supreme were (and still often are) dry counties, so drinks weren't always part of the Southern food experience, but that all changes at events like pig pickin', backyard 'cues, tailgating, and the like, because people always figured out a way to sneak some liquid fun into the mix. But even if you don't drink booze as a matter of personal choice—not due to state-mandated legislature—we have an array of Southern beverages for you. Whether you're buying Cheerwine—a cherry-flavored cola—in the store or using our included recipes for the perfect glass of refreshing homemade, never-from-concentrate lemonade, your mouth will thank you.

Last, but certainly not least, we've got sweet tea covered. If you're in the South, you'll see this beverage on every single menu, and you should pronounce it as any proper Southerner would: sweetea (make sure to include a drawl in there). Don't be shocked by the amount of sugar in this drink—it's called sweet tea for a reason. The trick is to add the sugar while the tea is brewing and still hot, so it's not all granulated at the bottom of your glass. And just as "barbecue" in North Carolina means pulled or chopped pork, "tea" in the South refers specifically to sweet tea. Mix it with lemonade and you get the Arnold Palmer. The Charleston A.P. is the alcohol-bolstered version of that same drink.

Whatever you choose to pour in your cup, just make sure it's always filled. An empty glass is akin to sacrilege at any Southern bash—a notion we hold near and dear to our heart at Brother Jimmy's.

Note: When we talk about using a shaker for the mixing of the libations, we're referring to a 30-ounce metal shaker. These are available at any home goods store.

LEMONADE

Nothing beats a tall glass of ice-cold lemonade on a hot, hazy summer afternoon. Be sure to garnish with a lemon wedge.

MAKES six 8-ounce drinks

1 cup room-temperature water

¾ cup sugar

1 cup fresh lemon juice (about 6 lemons)

4 cups cold water

Lemon wedges for garnish

1 Combine the 1 cup of room temperature water and sugar in a small saucepan and place over medium heat. Bring to a simmer and cook until the sugar dissolves, 1 to 2 minutes.

2 Meanwhile, combine the lemon juice and cold water in a pitcher. Pour the syrup into the pitcher.

3 Mix and serve over ice, with lemon wedges.

SWEET TEA

The quintessential Southern drink.

8 cups water

1½ cups sugar

6 regular-size tea bags (about ½ ounce)

Mint sprigs for garnish (optional)

MAKES one 64-ounce pitcher

In a saucepan over medium heat, bring the water and sugar to a simmer. Once the sugar has dissolved, bring the mixture to a boil, then remove from heat. Place the tea bags into the hot water–sugar mixture and let steep for about 15 minutes. Pour the mixture into a pitcher. Press the tea bags against the side of the pitcher with a wooden spoon to extract all the liquid, then remove. Store in the refrigerator and drink within a few days. Serve over ice and garnish with a sprig of mint if you like.

CAROLINA COOLER

MAKES 1 drink

This is what we call our "spiked" lemonade. It's a vodka- and lemonade-based drink with blue curaçao for that bright color. It's refreshing and light, perfect for when you're looking for a sweet and sour drink.

2 ounces vodka

¾ ounce blue curaçao

Lemonade (page 52)

Splash of Sprite for topping

Lemon twist for garnish

. . . .

In an ice-filled 16-ounce mason jar, combine the vodka and curaçao. Fill three-quarters with lemonade. Add a splash of Sprite, place a shaker on top of the jar, and shake well. Garnish with the lemon twist. By the way, be sure to add just a splash of Sprite. If you put too much in before you shake, it'll explode.

LOUISVILLE LEMONADE

MAKES 1 drink

This is the Kentucky take on the famous whiskey-spiked lemonade concoction known as Lynchburg Lemonade, named after the hometown of Jack Daniel's, which is featured in the original drink.

2 ounces Kentucky bourbon, such as Maker's Mark

1 ounce triple sec

50/50 mix of store-bought sour mix (we prefer Lemon-X brand) and Sprite

1 lemon wedge for garnish

. . . .

In an iced 16-ounce mason jar, combine the bourbon and triple sec. Fill with the sour mix and Sprite. Place a shaker on top of the jar and shake well. Garnish with the lemon wedge.

PALMETTO PUNCH

A Carolina version of a Rum Runner made with spiced rum, coconut rum, fruit juice, and a Myers's float, this drink is perfect for those looking for a sweet tropical taste with a kick.

2 ounces spiced rum

¾ ounce coconut rum

Splash of pineapple juice

Splash of grenadine

Orange juice for topping

Dark rum, such as Myers's, for floating on top

1 orange wedge for garnish

MAKES 1 drink

. . . .

Combine the rums, pineapple juice, and grenadine in an iced 16-ounce mason jar. Top with orange juice. Place a shaker over the jar and shake well. Float the dark rum on top. Garnish with the orange wedge.

THE CHARLESTON A.P.

This is the Brother Jimmy's alcoholic version of the Arnold Palmer (A.P.). This cocktail has never met a mouth that didn't appreciate it.

2 ounces sweet tea vodka

Lemonade (page 52)

1 lemon wedge for garnish

MAKES 1 drink

. . . .

Pour the sweet tea vodka into an ice-filled 16-ounce mason jar. Fill the remainder of the jar with lemonade. Cover the jar with a shaker and shake well. Garnish with the lemon wedge. Top this with Sweet Tea (page 52) for a sweeter cocktail.

PARTY CUPS OF CHOICE: Where home parties are concerned, Solo cups have long dominated the alcohol container department. They're cheap and disposable, come in team colors, and work much better than a pint glass if you're playing flip cup at halftime during the big game. But there are some other options. I'm a big fan of a trough, but something tells me you guys won't want to slurp out your booze from one, so how about trying mason jars? They come cheap, and we serve most of our liquids in them at Brother Jimmy's restaurants. You can pick them up at Walmart or your local hardware store, and it adds a cool aesthetic to the room when all your guests are holding mason jars filled with brightly colored drinks. Plus it'll cut down on stacks of half-full plastic cups littered around the room at the end of the night.

PALMETTO PUNCH

LOUISVILLE LEMONADE

BATTLE OF ANTIETAM
BLOODY MARY

CHARLESTON A.P.

MYRTLE MARGARITA
ON THE ROCKS

Kosher salt for rimming the glass (optional)

2 ounces silver tequila

1 ounce triple sec

1 ounce Rose's Lime Juice

2 ounces store-bought sour mix (we prefer Lemon-X brand)

Splash of orange juice

Lime wedge for garnish

MAKES 1 drink

Our margarita is made with lots of tequila and triple sec, sour mix, a drop of orange juice, and a vigorous shake.

If you'd like a salted rim, rim a 16-ounce mason jar in salt (see below). In another mason jar, add ice and then the tequila, triple sec, and Rose's Lime Juice. Add the sour mix and orange juice. Place a shaker on top of the jar and shake well. Pour into the rimmed glass, if using, or serve directly from the mason jar, garnished with the lime wedge.

And if you'd like a frozen margarita, just pour it all into a blender along with an extra scoop of ice, and mix to your heart's content.

HOW TO RIM A GLASS: There's no reason you can't look like a bartending pro at your next party. I personally like to watch *Cocktail* and emulate Tom Cruise's slick moves during parties at my pen, but you don't have to juggle flaming bottles to look suave. There are the little things that can make all the difference, such as rimming a glass properly. To start, place the dry rimmer ingredients in a shallow saucer. The next step is to moisten the outside edge of the glass with a sticky substance so that the rimmer will stick to it. You can do this several different ways. If citrus is used in the drink, cut a slit in a wedge of the same type of citrus used in the drink, and slide the wedge around the rim of the glass. Or you can pour one of the sugary ingredients used in the drink, such as triple sec, or 2:1 simple syrup (page 63), in a saucer, and moisten the rim by dipping the glass into the sugary liquid. Then hold the glass by its base at a 45-degree angle and allow the rim to rest on the dry rimmer ingredients, rotating the glass until the whole rim is coated.

TRASH CAN PUNCH

The ultimate in party drinking, this humongous drink is served in a 2½-gallon glass mason jar and serves about twenty people. It is a rum-based punch and packs just that—a powerful punch. Made with an entire bottle of white rum, Hawaiian Punch, sour mix, and orange juice, the finished concoction is topped off with a floater of Myers's, Captain Morgan, and Malibu rums. Don't forget a ladle and some plastic cups for those who don't wish to sip it out of the jar.

Fill a 2½-gallon mason jar with ice. Add the white rum, Hawaiian Punch, sour mix, and orange juice and stir to combine. Float the dark, spiced, and coconut rums over the top of the drink. Add a bunch of festive straws and serve.

1 (750-ml) bottle white rum

1 (46-ounce) can Hawaiian Punch

3 cups store-bought sour mix (we prefer Lemon-X brand)

1 quart orange juice

1 ounce dark rum, such as Myers's

1 ounce spiced rum, such as Captain Morgan

1 ounce coconut rum, such as Malibu

MAKES 2½ gallons

SOUTHERN RED SANGRIA

MAKES 1 (64-ounce) pitcher

This is a traditional red sangria made with apples and oranges. It's perfect for large groups and great for picnics or at a backyard barbecue.

¾ cup triple sec

½ cup cognac or brandy

½ cup orange juice

1 large apple, cut into ½-inch pieces

1 orange, cut into thin wedges, plus extra for garnish

1 bottle Spanish dry red wine, chilled

. . . .

In a pitcher, combine 1 cup of ice, the triple sec, cognac, orange juice, and fruit. Pour in the wine. Stir and serve in ice-filled wine glasses with an orange wedge.

WHITE PEACH SANGRIA

MAKES 1 (64-ounce) pitcher

Same deal as the red sangria, only this time we're using grapes and some peach schnapps.

¾ cup peach schnapps

½ cup brandy

1 cup seedless green grapes, cut in half

2 peaches, cut into thin wedges

About ¾ bottle Sauvignon Blanc, chilled

½ cup Sprite

. . . .

In a pitcher, combine the peach schnapps, brandy, fruit, and 1 cup of ice. Fill with wine up to 1 inch from the top of the pitcher. Top with the Sprite and stir. Serve in ice-filled wine glasses.

CHARLOTTE TEA

This is Brother Jimmy's version of a traditional Long Island Iced Tea; the difference is we add coconut rum to the mix. Watch out because this one is very strong.

. . . .

In an iced 16-ounce mason jar, combine the vodka, gin, tequila, coconut rum, triple sec, and sour mix . Place a shaker on top of the jar and shake well. Top with a splash of Coke (or add more Coke and cut down on the sour mix for a sweeter drink) and garnish with the lemon wedge.

- ½ ounce vodka
- ½ ounce gin
- ½ ounce silver tequila
- ½ ounce coconut rum
- ½ ounce triple sec
- 50/50 mix store-bought sour mix (we prefer Lemon-X brand)
- Splash of Coke
- Lemon wedge for garnish

MAKES 1 drink

HOW TO CUT A WEDGE: Let's talk about cutting fruit for garnishes. If you're slicing a lemon or lime, the procedure's pretty much the same. You want to hold the fruit and cut off the tips at both ends. Stand it up on its now-flat bottom. Cut it in half vertically. Place the skin side down and cut a slit lengthwise through most of the fruit. This is the slit that you'll place on the lip of the glass. Now, flip 'er over and slice through the skin side crosswise to make 4 or 5 individual wedges. For an orange, we're gonna have to break out some math terms. Start the same way you do with lemons and limes and cut the tips off each end of the orange. Now that you have a flat bottom, cut it in half vertically. Then you want to bisect the halves, then bisect the quarters. Give each of the pieces a crosswise slit and you're left with 90-degree quarters that'll hang nicely off the glass.

DRUNKEN SAILOR

A simple mix of spiced rum and Cheerwine. This is always a hit with the ladies.

2 ounces spiced rum

Cheerwine

1 maraschino cherry for garnish

. . . .

Pour the rum into an iced 16-ounce mason jar. Fill with Cheerwine. Stir and garnish with the maraschino cherry.

MAKES 1 drink

ABOUT CHEERWINE: This popular North Carolina bottled soda with its signature wild cherry flavor, burgundy color, and lovely effervescence (it's more highly carbonated than most sodas) was created in 1917 by L. D. Peeler, a general store owner. (Visit www.cheerwine.com to learn more about the Cheerwine story and to purchase bottles or cans of it.) We serve it straight up at all of our Brother Jimmy's locations, use it as a mixer in drinks, and even make an ice cream float with it.

HURRICANE

MAKES 1 drink

This is a classic New Orleans concoction, so it goes well with any seafood medley or boil. Plus you get to pour it in that nifty Hurricane glass. (If you don't own a Hurricane glass, any 14- to 20-ounce glass will do.)

1 ounce vodka

¼ ounce grenadine

1 ounce light rum

½ ounce 151-proof rum

1 ounce Amaretto liqueur

1 ounce triple sec

Grapefruit juice

Pineapple juice

A couple of chunks of pineapple or grapefruit, with a slice cut into them, to hang from the rim, for garnish (optional)

. . . .

Fill a Hurricane glass three-quarters full with ice. Pour in all of the ingredients except the juices and garnishes in the order listed. Fill the balance with equal parts grapefruit and pineapple juice. Stir to combine and garnish with a chunk of grapefruit or pineapple if you like.

CHERRY
BOMB

Everyone loves a bomb-style drink now and again. Just remember when filling the pint glass to leave plenty of space because you'll displace a lot of the energy drink when dropping in the shot glass. And you can swap the cherry for any other flavored vodka to keep the flavors fresh.

1 shot glass filled with cherry-flavored vodka

1 pint glass half-filled with any energy drink

MAKES 1 drink

Drop the shot glass into the pint glass and chug as fast as you can.

SWAMP · WATER

1 liter vodka

½ liter melon liqueur

½ gallon store-bought sour mix (we prefer Lemon-X)

1½ (46-ounce) cans pineapple juice

1 (32-ounce) bottle Sprite

1 (32-ounce) pitcher water

3¾ ounces grenadine for the plastic gators

MAKES 2½ gallons (or enough for five 64-ounce fishbowls)

Our signature drink hasn't changed in twenty years; it's what people come to Brother Jimmy's for. Swamp Water is a vodka and melon liqueur–based punch with pineapple sour mix, juice, and Sprite. We serve it in a 64-ounce fishbowl with an 11-inch rubber alligator filled with bright red grenadine and lots of festive colored straws for sharing. When you serve it, turn the alligator over into the fishbowl; it will look like the alligator is dying and bleeding into the swamp. (Check your local novelty store for the alligators.) This makes 2½ gallons, so it's perfect for your party, since it'll serve about twenty people. If you want less of it, just cut the numbers down proportionally.

Combine all the ingredients in a large bowl, then pour everything evenly into five 64-ounce fishbowls filled with ice. Place multicolored straws in each fishbowl and pour ¾ ounces of the grenadine in each plastic gator.

THE GRAND
STRAND
MARGARITA

Our top shelf "Cadillac" margarita, named after the glorious coastline of North and South Carolina—the Grand Strand. The difference between this margarita and a regular margarita is top-shelf silver tequila, Grand Marnier, fresh lime juice, and simple syrup.

. . . .

If you'd like a salted rim, rim a 16-ounce mason jar (see page 56). In another mason jar, muddle 8 lime wedges (see page 59). Fill with ice and add the tequila, Grand Marnier, and simple syrup. Place a shaker on top of the jar and shake well. Pour into the rimmed glass, if using, or serve directly from the mason jar, garnished with a lime wedge.

Kosher salt for rimming the glass (optional)

8 lime wedges, plus 1 for garnish

2 ounces good-quality silver tequila

¾ ounce Grand Marnier

Splash of simple syrup (see below)

MAKES 1 drink

SIMPLE
SYRUP

MAKES 2 cups

There's nothing easier to make than simple syrup. We use a 2:1 ratio.

2 cups sugar

1 cup water

. . . .

Combine the sugar and water in a small saucepan, place over medium heat, and bring to a boil. Stir until the sugar dissolves, then remove from the heat and cool. Store in a clean glass bottle or jar with a tight-fitting lid in the refrigerator. It'll keep for up to 1 month.

OUR ST. PATTY'S

IRISH CAR BOMB

This staple "bomb"-style drink is infamous, even though it's not typically consumed in the motherland.

½ ounce Irish cream liqueur, such as Baileys

½ ounce Irish whiskey, such as Jameson

1 pint glass three-quarters filled with Guinness Stout

. . . .

Combine the Irish cream liqueur and whiskey in a shot glass. Drop the shot into the glass with the Guinness Stout and slam it back.

MAKES 1 drink

DUBLIN HANDSHAKE

Don't feel like being all violent with an Irish Car Bomb? Give peace a chance with the Dublin Handshake.

½ ounce Irish cream liqueur, such as Baileys

½ ounce Irish whiskey, such as Jameson

¾ ounce sloe gin

. . . .

Combine the ingredients in an iced shaker. Shake well and strain into an iced rocks glass. Remember to hug your neighbor while you enjoy it.

MAKES 1 drink

GREEN BEER

We serve this up at our Brother Jimmy's locations on St. Patty's Day and find our guests love to play beer pong with it. Plus, green beer just looks cool. Added bonus to green beer: Spill it on a green shirt and no one will notice.

Any pale beer
Green food coloring

. . . .

Simply add three drops of green food coloring per pint of beer and you're good to go.

ST. PATTY'S DAY DRINKS: I LOVE ST. PATRICK'S DAY. It's the one time of year when everyone acts like a pig, so I fit right in. Whether you're stuffing your face full of delicious food or downing drinks like they're going out of style, the name of the game on this day is excess—something we swine know well. Here, you'll find some of our favorite St. Patty's cocktails and shooters, as well as how to turn your beer green.

DAY DRINKS

PICKLEBACK

This is among the simplest yet tastiest of shots.

1 ounce Irish whiskey

1 ounce pickle juice

. . . .

Take the shot of whiskey. Then take the shot of pickle juice. Then grin in satisfaction.

MAKES 1 shot

THE DANCING LEPRECHAUN

This drink keeps the whiskey flowing and the legs jigging.

1½ ounces Irish whiskey, such as Jameson

¾ ounce Drambuie

¾ ounce lemon juice

Splash of ginger ale

1 lemon twist for garnish

. . . .

Combine all of the ingredients in an iced shaker. Shake well, then strain into an iced highball glass. Garnish with the lemon twist and then commence with the dancing. We recommend a jig of some sort.

MAKES 1 drink

IRISH TRASH CAN

If Ireland had a Long Island, this would be its namesake drink. This drink is best served in a collins glass. Any tall, slender glass with a 12-ounce capacity will work.

½ ounce gin

½ ounce light rum

½ ounce vodka

½ ounce peach schnapps

½ ounce blue curaçao

½ ounce triple sec

1 (5-ounce) can Red Bull Energy Drink

. . . .

Fill a large collins glass with ice, add all the liquors, and stir thoroughly. Last, open and drop in a full can of Red Bull upside-down. The can will float at first, then as the energy drink empties, it will slowly sink, turning your drink green as it does.

MAKES 1 drink

BRUNCH DRINKS

Because you have to start the party early some days.

RISE & SHINE

This is a screwdriver with a twist. It can be served in a mason jar or a fishbowl.

FOR A SINGLE DRINK:

2 ounces vodka

Orange juice

Grenadine for drizzling

. . . .

Pour the vodka into an iced 16-ounce mason jar and fill with the orange juice. Add a drizzle of grenadine and stir to combine.

FOR A 64-OUNCE FISHBOWL:

8 ounces vodka

Orange juice

Grenadine for drizzling

. . . .

Fill a fishbowl with ice. Add the vodka, then fill with orange juice. Add a drizzle of grenadine and stir to combine.

FIZZY PEACH

This is a peach-and champagne–based drink that goes perfectly with brunch. The fruit will settle on the bottom of the glass, but that's okay; it will be a surprise treat at the end of the drink.

2 ounces peach puree (either puree peaches in a food processor or mince the fruit by hand)

4 ounces champagne

. . . .

Put the peach puree in the bottom of a champagne flute. Fill with champagne. Drink with your pinky extended at all times.

MAKES 1 drink

NOTE: You can easily make the Fizzy Peach into a Mimosa by substituting the peach puree for orange juice.

HOW TO MUDDLE: When I was a tiny piglet (and wore boots!), I used to excel in muddling—because my sty was always full of mud. But when I grew up, I found out that muddling is actually used to extract and combine flavors. Who knew? Sometimes ingredients are muddled with sugar, which acts as an abrasive. Ingredients are placed in the bottom of a mixing glass, heavy-bottomed serving glass, or cocktail shaker and are firmly pressed with the flat end of the muddler until all of the juices are extracted and the sugar is dissolved. Herbs will become transparent when sufficiently muddled. And what, exactly, is a muddler? It's a long pestle, from about 8 to 12 inches in length, made of wood, metal, or plastic. If you don't have muddler, in a pinch you can use a wooden spoon handle.

BLOODY BEER

A nice simple mix of Budweiser, tomato juice, Tabasco, Worcestershire, and fresh lime juice.

Brother Jimmy's Bloody Mary Rimming Spice for rimming (page 68)

2 ounces tomato juice

3 dashes Tabasco sauce

2 dashes Worcestershire sauce

1 lime wedge

Budweiser beer

. . . .

Rim a pint glass with the Bloody Mary spice. Add the tomato juice, Tabasco sauce, and Worcestershire sauce. Squeeze the lime wedge into the glass, fill with Budweiser, and stir.

MAKES 1 drink

MINT JULEP (HAIR OF THE DOG)

A classic Mint Julep with Maker's Mark bourbon and fresh mint, this drink is refreshing any time of the day.

8 to 12 fresh mint leaves

1 ounce Simple Syrup (page 63)

2 ounces Kentucky bourbon, such as Maker's Mark

Soda water

Mint sprig for garnish

. . . .

Place the mint leaves and simple syrup in a 16-ounce mason jar. Muddle the mint (see above). Fill with ice and add the bourbon. Securely fit a metal shaker over the top of the mason jar and shake well. Top with soda water and garnish with the mint sprig.

MAKES 1 drink

BLOODY MARY

Brother Jimmy's Bloody Mary
Rimming Spice (recipe follows)

2 ounces vodka

Brother Jimmy's Bloody Mary
Mix (recipe follows)

1 lemon wedge

FOR GARNISH:

3 Pickled Chipotle String Beans
(page 45)

3 green olives

1 (6-inch-long) celery stalk

1 lemon wedge

MAKES 1 drink

A classic Bloody Mary made from scratch with tomato juice, horseradish, celery salt, black pepper, hot sauce, and Worchester sauce. Then we add the vodka, our special "rimming spice"—celery seed, kosher salt, and Old Bay—and a festive array of garnishes. For those looking for some extra heat, you can pick up our Blazin' Jalapeño Stuffed Olives from our website; they go great in here.

Rim a 16-ounce mason jar with the Bloody Mary Rimming Spice. Fill another mason jar or a shaker with ice, add the vodka, and squeeze in one lemon wedge. Fill with Bloody Mary Mix and shake well. Pour into the rimmed glass and garnish with the Pickled Chipotle String Beans, olives, celery stalk, and lemon wedge.

BROTHER JIMMY'S BLOODY MARY RIMMING SPICE

2 tablespoons Old Bay

1 tablespoon celery salt

4 teaspoons kosher salt

Combine all the ingredients in a shallow dish and mix well. Store in a covered container in a cool, dry place.

MAKES just over ¼ cup

BROTHER JIMMY'S BLOODY MARY MIX

1 (46-ounce) can tomato juice

¼ cup prepared white horseradish

1¾ teaspoons Frank's Red Hot Sauce

1¾ teaspoons Worcestershire sauce

1¾ teaspoons celery salt

1 teaspoon ground black pepper

Combine all the ingredients in a large pitcher or jar. Keep in an airtight container in the refrigerator for up to 1 week.

MAKES about 6 cups

SHOOTERS

Because sometimes, good things come in (powerfully) small packages. All of our shots are served in a 1-ounce shot glass.

RED NECK

½ ounce Jack Daniel's
¼ ounce melon liqueur
¼ ounce cranberry juice

Combine all the ingredients in an iced shaker. Shake to combine and strain into a shot glass.

. . . .

DOUBLE BARREL

Fill a shot glass halfway with **Wild Turkey American Honey.** Fill the remaining half with **orange juice.**

. . . .

RED HOT SHOT

Fill a shot glass halfway with **Red Stag** (a black cherry–infused bourbon created by Jim Beam). Fill the remaining half with **cinnamon liqueur.**

. . . .

PRAIRIE FIRE

Fill a shot glass with any type of **tequila.** Add a dash of **Tabasco** or other hot sauce to the top. Your mouth will literally be on fire.

COUNTRY APPLE

This shot is always a hit because it tastes just like a Jolly Rancher apple candy.

⅓ ounce bourbon
⅓ ounce DeKuyper Sour Apple Pucker Schnapps
⅓ ounce cranberry juice

Combine all the ingredients in an iced shaker. Shake to combine and strain into a shot glass.

. . . .

SOUTHERN SHAG

⅓ ounce Southern Comfort
⅓ ounce Amaretto liqueur
⅓ ounce pineapple juice

Combine all the ingredients in an iced shaker. Shake to combine and strain into a shot glass.

WHITE LIGHTNING

⅓ ounce gin
⅓ ounce Sprite
⅓ ounce Wildberry Pucker

Combine all the ingredients in an iced shaker. Shake to combine and strain into a shot glass.

. . . .

TIC-TAC SHOT

Fill a shot glass halfway with any **orange-flavored rum.** Fill the remaining half with **Red Bull.**

. . . .

PINK FLAMINGO

½ ounce vodka
¼ ounce triple sec
Splash of cranberry juice
Juice from 2 lime wedges

Combine all the ingredients in an iced shaker. Shake to combine and strain into a shot glass.

CHAPTER Nº 4

STARTERS

THE CHEERING DURING

FINAL FOUR GAMES AT BROTHER JIMMY'S IS

so loud that you can hear it from the sidewalk. Inside, a quick survey of the energized room reveals a sea of uniformed color, thanks to super fans decked out in their team's jerseys, hats, headbands, and more. It's one of our biggest days in the restaurant because alumni from ACC (Atlantic Coast Conference) and SEC (Southeastern Conference) and more know to flock here to watch their teams in the manner they were accustomed to during college. It's like the packed room is filled with numerous versions of that crazy friend we all know, the one who always painted his stomach and went shirtless to every game—even in the dead of winter. The camaraderie is so thick, it's almost palpable—just the way we like it.

While the end of March Madness plays out on our flat screens, we're in the midst of playing good hosts, making sure the beer is flowing, that our fishbowls are filled and the toy alligators filled with an extra shot are floating atop them. And sure, booze is an important necessity to any solid Final Four viewing—which explains why we go through nearly 9,000 cans of beer and 11,000 pints of brew each Final Four week—but we're also serving up an incredible amount of fine finger fare. We're plating up 2,200 pounds of drool-inducing ribs. We're pulling 3,500 pounds of savory, slow-cooked pork and piling it high atop your plate. We're slicing 1,900 pounds of smoked brisket. We're also pouring nearly 300 gallons of our trademark 'cue sauces. All of which gives you the fuel to shout even louder when your team drains that oh-so-crucial three pointer right before the buzzer.

This chapter will teach you all the fundamentals to bringing the same vibe, energy, and atmosphere of the Final Four experience from a Brother Jimmy's right into your living room. We've honed the art of entertaining over the years, and with our recipes, tips, and tricks, there's no reason your home can't be the setting for an equally amazing time for the Final Four. Our formula for fun is pretty simple: solid drinks, good tunes cranking during the game's downtimes, and perfect down-home Southern cooking. All you need to do is provide the TV for the games and your own crew of smack-talking friends.

Our stance is that during game time, appetizers are more than merely something to whet your appetite. These aren't appe-teasers (you should probably reconsider your friendship with anyone who uses that word in earnest); they're a hearty meal on their own merits. Who needs a formal, nutritionally balanced plate of grub when several baskets of fried food, scrumptious dips, and smoky sauces will more than adequately suffice?

Whipping up an array of treats can be easier than you would think. These aren't dishes you'll spend hours slaving away creating, though the finished products will taste like you did. They're simple enough for even the most novice of chefs to master quickly. From Spinach and Artichoke Dip to Perfect Peel-and-Eat Shrimp to Fried Green Tomatoes with Garlic Aioli, we've got you covered. When you're done here, you'll have enough plates to fill your counters and tables and offer a little slice of Southern heaven to your guests' palates. The only thing we really can't do is help you choose a winning bracket. You're on your own there, champ.

PLAYLIST

Remember your favorite songs from your college years? What better way to watch this year's NCAA championship than by firing up these classics? These are songs that everyone knows the words to, and that often end up in party-wide sing-alongs, right from the first refrain.

GREEN DAY
GOOD RIDDANCE

WEEZER
ISLAND IN THE SUN

NIRVANA
ALL APOLOGIES

COWBOY MOUTH
HOW DO YOU TELL SOMEONE

CUSTER
ONE MAN WRECKING MACHINE

O.A.R.
HEY GIRL

BEN FOLDS FIVE
SONG FOR THE DUMPED

BARENAKED LADIES
ONE WEEK

CRACKER
LOW

BLUES TRAVELER
RUN-AROUND

STEVIE RAY VAUGHAN
THE HOUSE IS ROCKIN'

CITIZEN COPE
I'VE SEEN BETTER DAYS

R.E.M.
RADIO FREE EUROPE

PEARL JAM
GIVEN TO FLY

WIDESPREAD PANIC
AIN'T LIFE GRAND

KID ROCK
WASTING TIME

THE SMITHEREENS
BEHIND THE WALL OF SLEEP

TALKING HEADS
TAKE ME TO THE RIVER

RYAN ADAMS
TO BE YOUNG

SUM 41
IN TOO DEEP

FRIED GREEN TOMATOES

WITH GARLIC AIOLI

Steal a scene from the namesake movie, but skip the lard and opt for vegetable oil, as it'll be healthier for you. These breaded and fried green tomatoes, served with a creamy garlic aioli, are the perfect afternoon snack or dinner side.

1 **Make the garlic aioli:** In a medium bowl, combine all the ingredients.

2 **Make the fried green tomatoes:** Slice the tomatoes into ³⁄₈-inch-thick slices.

3 In a shallow dish, combine the breadcrumbs, cornmeal, salt, pepper, and celery salt. In a separate shallow dish, beat the egg with the buttermilk. Place the flour in another shallow dish.

4 In a large heavy frying pan (cast iron works well) over medium heat, bring about 1 inch of oil up to 325°F.

5 Start by dredging the tomatoes in the flour, shaking off as much excess flour as possible. Next, pass them through the egg mixture and then dredge them in the breadcrumb mixture.

6 Once you have all the tomatoes well coated, start frying in batches for 1 to 2 minutes each, until they are golden brown on both sides. Transfer the fried tomatoes to paper towels to drain excess oil while continuing to fry new batches. (Always make sure you have about 1 inch of oil—add more if necessary—and keep the temperature at 325°F.) Serve with the garlic aioli.

FOR THE GARLIC AIOLI:

1 cup Hellman's mayonnaise

1½ teaspoons fresh lemon juice

⅛ teaspoon kosher salt

3 tablespoons finely chopped garlic

1 tablespoon Worcestershire sauce

FOR THE FRIED GREEN TOMATOES:

3 or 4 green tomatoes

½ cup plain breadcrumbs

½ cup cornmeal

¾ teaspoon kosher salt

1½ teaspoons ground black pepper

1½ teaspoons celery salt

1 large egg

½ cup buttermilk

½ cup all-purpose flour

Vegetable oil for frying

SERVES 4 to 6

FRICKLES

FRIED GREEN
TOMATOES WITH
GARLIC AIOLI

HUSH PUPPIES WITH
MAPLE BUTTER

HUSH PUPPIES
WITH MAPLE BUTTER

The cayenne gives these puppies a little kick, which the creamy sweetness of the maple butter mellows. Hush puppies are put on the table straight away, much like a Southern version of a bread basket, so you can give your guests a treat right when they arrive. Serve hot with maple butter. (See "Deep-Frying 101" on page 77 if you're a first-time fryer.) By the way, this sweetened maple butter goes great on everything from pancakes to cornbread, so don't worry if you have any leftover—you can freeze it, too.

1 **Make the maple butter:** In a large bowl, beat together the butter and maple syrup until incorporated. Set aside at room temperature. (If you make the maple butter ahead and have stored it in the fridge, bring it to room temperature before serving.)

2 **Make the hush puppies:** Heat 6 inches of oil to 325°F in a deep-fryer or heavy-bottomed stockpot. While the oil is heating, lightly beat the eggs in a large bowl. Whisk in the baking powder. Add the buttermilk and mix well. Add the oil and onion.

3 In a separate bowl, combine the cornmeal, flour, sugar, salt, cayenne, and granulated onion. Add the dry ingredients to the bowl with the wet ingredients; mix to incorporate, but don't overmix. Refrigerate until ready to use.

4 Carefully drop heaping tablespoons of the batter into the hot oil. (In the restaurant we use a ¾-ounce scoop.) Don't overcrowd the pot. Cook until golden brown, 3 to 5 minutes.

5 Using the deep-fryer's wire basket, a slotted spoon, or a spider, remove the hush puppies to paper towels to absorb extra oil or drain on a wire rack. Serve with the maple butter.

FOR THE MAPLE BUTTER:

1 cup (2 sticks) unsalted butter, at room temperature

¼ cup maple syrup

FOR THE HUSH PUPPIES:

2 large eggs

1 tablespoon baking powder

2 cups buttermilk

5 tablespoons vegetable oil

¾ cup diced Spanish onion

2 cups cornmeal

2¾ cups all-purpose flour

¼ cup sugar

¾ teaspoon kosher salt

½ teaspoon cayenne pepper

1 ½ teaspoons granulated onion

About 5 cups canola oil for deep-frying

MAKES about 2 dozen

FRICKLES

FOR THE HORSERADISH SAUCE:

½ cup plus 2 tablespoons Hellman's mayonnaise

3 tablespoons prepared white horseradish

2 tablespoons Worcestershire sauce

2 tablespoons sour cream

FOR THE FRICKLES:

About 4 cups canola oil for deep-frying

1 cup yellow mustard, such as French's

1 cup golden ale

3 to 4 cups panko (Japanese breadcrumbs)

1 cup all-purpose flour

48 good-quality pickle chips (we use dill), well drained

SERVES 6

Our famous fried pickles are a hugely popular item in our restaurants. We think the beer in the batter is what makes them so good. You get the pickle and mustard flavors because they're so dominant, but the beer complements them nicely. We serve our frickles with a creamy horseradish dipping sauce. (See "Deep-Frying 101" on page 77 if you're a first-time fryer.)

1 **Make the horseradish sauce:** Combine all the ingredients in a small bowl. Cover and refrigerate until ready to use.

2 **Make the frickles:** In a deep-fryer or heavy-bottomed stockpot, heat 4 to 5 inches of oil over medium heat to 350°F. While the oil is heating, combine the mustard and beer in a shallow bowl. Place the panko and flour in two separate shallow bowls.

3 Pat the pickle chips with paper towels to get as much excess liquid off them as you can, then toss them in the flour (you might want to do this in batches). Shake off excess flour, then drop them into the mustard-beer mixture. Move the pickles to the panko and toss well to coat.

4 When all the pickles are coated, fry them in batches until they turn golden brown, 2 to 3 minutes. Using the deep-fryer's wire basket, a slotted spoon, or a spider, remove the frickles to paper towels to absorb extra oil or drain on a wire rack.

5 Serve the frickles hot with the horseradish sauce.

DRINKS: Cans or bottles of beer will always do in a pinch and a case of beer should be a staple resident in the fridge of any Final Four party, but there's no need to limit yourself to only the hops. We've got some solid drink concoctions to suit any liquor profile. Mix up a pitcher or two and keep them on hand as an alternative to a glass of brew. As an added bonus, they're mighty colorful, so if you're really into team spirit, you'd best be gulping a drink that matches your team's jersey.

SWAMP WATER

Swamp Water is a vodka and melon liquor–based punch with some fruit juice and Sprite in the mix. When we serve it in the restaurants, it's also got a lovely gator floating on the top with a hidden surprise of grenadine (page 62).

CAROLINA COOLER

This is what we call our "spiked" lemonade. It's a vodka and lemonade–based drink with blue curaçao for that Carolina Blue that reminds everyone of our North Carolina roots (page 53).

DEEP-FRYING 101: EVERYONE LOVES DEEP-FRIED FOODS, but deep-frying at home can be intimidating to some. With these basic steps, you'll find that it's really *not* hard to prepare perfect golden-browned bites at home—foods that are delicious, light, and not greasy. The key to deep-frying is to heat the oil until it is sufficiently hot, and then to maintain the correct temperature during cooking. That's how you ensure the grub isn't greasy.

- Use a proper frying vessel, ideally outfitted with a fry basket. If you don't have a deep-fryer, use a deep pot with high sides to allow for several inches of headroom.

- Use a neutral-flavored oil with a high smoke point. We use canola oil.

- Make sure the oil is sufficiently deep to completely submerge the foods in the oil. The amount needed will depend on the size and shape of the food, but generally about 3 inches of oil will be enough. For safety, never fill a pot more than halfway.

- Make sure the oil is good and hot before adding the food. The temperature we use for most deep-fried foods is 350°F. To check the temp, use a deep-fry thermometer (these handy devices come with a built-in clip that can be attached to the side of your pot).

- Fry the food in small batches to keep the temperature of the oil from fluctuating. (Every time you add a piece of food, it will lower the temperature of the oil.) Check the temp often to make sure the oil is hot enough, and moderate the heat as needed before adding the next batch of food.

- Occasionally turn the food to make sure it fries evenly on all sides.

- Remove foods from the fryer with a wire basket—the easiest method—or with a slotted spoon or wire-mesh spider.

- Drain foods on a wire rack set over a sheet pan or place on a board lined with some paper towels.

- When disposing of used oil, throw it out in the trash rather than down the drain.

SPINACH & ARTICHOKE

DIP

2 tablespoons olive oil

1 cup diced Spanish onion

2 tablespoons chopped garlic

½ teaspoon salt

½ teaspoon ground
black pepper

1 cup artichoke hearts (frozen)

6 ounces cream cheese,
softened

8 ounces frozen chopped
spinach, thawed

½ cup sour cream

2 cups grated Monterey Jack
cheese (about 8 ounces)

½ cup grated Parmesan cheese
(about 2 ounces)

SERVES 6 to 8

This is a nice and simple starter for a large group. For a fancier presentation, spread some on individual slices of grilled bread or pita. As a bonus, you'll be eating your spinach, which would make Popeye proud.

1 Preheat the oven to 350°F.

2 In a medium sauté pan, heat the oil over medium-low heat. Add the onion, garlic, salt, and pepper and sauté until the onion is soft and translucent.

3 Process the artichoke hearts in a food processor until very fine. Add the cream cheese and process until well incorporated.

4 Squeeze the excess liquid from the spinach (there will be a lot) and add to the food processor along with the sour cream and 1½ cups of the grated Monterey Jack cheese and the Parmesan cheese. Pulse in the food processor until combined.

5 Transfer the mixture to a baking dish and sprinkle with the remaining ½ cup Monterey Jack cheese. Bake for about 20 minutes, or until the top is lightly browned and bubbly.

6 Serve with tortilla chips, grilled bread, or pita bread.

PERFECT PEEL-&-EAT SHRIMP

WITH HOMEMADE COCKTAIL SAUCE

The extra kick of the Old Bay Seasoning and lemon makes these shrimp come alive in your mouth. Plus, it's always great fun to flick the tails at your friends. This recipe for cocktail sauce makes about 1½ cups, just the right amount for this quantity of shrimp.

1 Make the cocktail sauce: Combine all the ingredients in a small bowl. Cover and refrigerate until ready to use.

2 Make the shrimp: If using frozen shrimp, defrost them, but don't peel them.

3 Cut the lemons in half and squeeze the juice into a pot; add the squeezed lemon halves as well. Add the water, vinegar, Old Bay, bay leaves, and salt. Place over medium-high heat and bring to a boil.

4 Add the shrimp and cook for 2 minutes, until they turn opaque.

5 Remove the shrimp and cool to room temperature as quickly as possible by placing them flat on a tray with sides, then refrigerate until cold.

6 Toss the shrimp with additional lemon juice and Old Bay. Serve with the cocktail sauce and extra napkins.

FOR THE COCKTAIL SAUCE:

1 cup ketchup

¼ cup prepared white horseradish

4 teaspoons fresh lemon juice

¼ cup Frank's Red Hot Sauce

1 teaspoon Worcestershire sauce

FOR THE SHRIMP:

2 pounds unpeeled medium to jumbo shrimp (fresh or frozen)

2 lemons

6 cups water

1 cup white vinegar

3 tablespoons Old Bay

2 bay leaves

2 teaspoons kosher salt

TO SERVE:

6 tablespoons fresh lemon juice

2 tablespoons Old Bay

SERVES 4 to 6

BBQ NACHOS

½ cup BBQ Baked Beans with Smoked Pork (page 216)

1 large bag tortilla chips (at least 9 ounces)

1½ cups shredded cheddar cheese

⅔ cup Smoky BBQ Chili (page 98)

⅓ cup Charred Tomato Salsa (page 81)

⅓ cup guacamole (recipe follows)

¼ cup sour cream

SERVES 4 to 6

You can make this entire recipe from leftovers from other recipes in this book, or you can make all the components fresh. These are the portions we use in the restaurant, but by all means, feel free to up the salsa, guacamole, and sour cream amounts.

1 Preheat the oven to 350°F.

2 Place the BBQ Baked Beans on the bottom of a heatproof platter and scatter half of the tortilla chips on top. Place half of the cheese over the chips. Place the remaining chips on top, then ladle the chili over the chips. Spread the remaining shredded cheese evenly over the top.

3 Place in the oven and heat until all the cheese is melted, 15 to 20 minutes.

4 Top the plate with the Charred Tomato Salsa, guacamole, and sour cream in individual piles and serve.

FROM VEGGIE THE PIG

One of my favorite Final Four treats is BBQ Nachos. They're perfect because they're so simple to make, yet pack such a bold flavor. They're also ideal for sharing, provided none of your guests hog the plate for themselves. Bulk them up by adding some additional meat, but just remember, you don't have to stick to my delicious brethren to top them with a protein; shredded beef or chicken work equally well.

GUACAMOLE

2 large ripe avocados

¼ cup minced Spanish onion

¼ cup minced tomato

½ to 1 jalapeño, seeded and minced

3 tablespoons chopped fresh cilantro

2 tablespoons fresh lime juice

1 teaspoon salt

¼ teaspoon minced garlic

MAKES about 2 cups

1 Cut the avocados in half, remove the pit, scoop out the flesh, and place it in a bowl. With a firm whisk or potato masher, mash the avocado until it is relatively smooth.

2 Add the remaining ingredients and mix until well combined. Taste and adjust the seasoning if needed.

SHRIMP & CORN
FRITTERS
WITH CHARRED TOMATO SALSA

You can make these fritters bite-size for smaller gatherings or keep them large and serve them over greens for a light lunch. They taste better when you use locally grown corn and heirloom tomatoes. We've provided two ways to char tomatoes for the salsa. You can serve it warm or chilled, and it'll keep for about 3 days in the fridge.

1 **Make the salsa:** Preheat your grill to high. It's important that the grates be very clean. We like to place a chunk of soaked wood or a packet of soaked wood chips on the coals right before placing the tomatoes on—but it's not necessary. When your grill is very hot, oil the hot grate. If you don't have a grill or prefer to use a pan, heat a cast-iron pan over medium-high heat until it's just about smoking.

2 Core the tomatoes and cut them in half. Toss with the oil and sprinkle with salt and pepper. Char the tomatoes on each side until blackened a bit, then flip. Remove from the grill or pan and cool. Chop the tomatoes, put them in a large bowl, and add the remaining ingredients.

3 **Make the fritters:** Cut the corn off the cob and place in a large bowl. Chop the shrimp into small pieces, but do not mince them. Add the shrimp to the corn. Add the remaining ingredients, except the canola oil, and mix well.

4 In a heavy-bottomed frying pan (cast iron works well), heat ⅛ to ¼ inch of oil over medium heat. Check the temperature of the oil with a drop of water; it should sizzle when the oil is hot enough.

5 Using a ¼-cup measure, carefully place mounds of the fritter batter into the pan and flatten slightly. Do not overcrowd. When they start to look golden brown (after about 2 minutes), gently flip them and cook for another 2 to 3 minutes. Remove and drain on paper towels. Repeat with remaining batter. Serve with the Charred Tomato Salsa.

FOR THE CHARRED TOMATO SALSA:

2 pounds ripe but still firm height-of-summer tomatoes

2 tablespoons olive oil

Salt and ground black pepper, to taste

½ cup minced Spanish onion

¼ cup chopped fresh cilantro

½ teaspoon Chipotle Puree (page 32)

1 teaspoon kosher salt

FOR THE FRITTERS:

2 ears corn

1 pound medium shrimp, peeled and deveined

¼ cup minced red pepper

½ cup thinly sliced scallion

3 tablespoons chopped fresh cilantro

1 teaspoon kosher salt

3 tablespoons all-purpose flour

2 large eggs, lightly beaten

1 teaspoon smoked sweet paprika

¼ teaspoon baking soda

½ teaspoon ground black pepper

Canola oil for frying

MAKES 12 fritters

APPLEWOOD-SMOKED-BACON
DEVILED EGGS

6 slices applewood-smoked bacon

12 large eggs

3 scallions, green parts only

½ teaspoon salt

¼ teaspoon ground black pepper

¼ cup Hellman's mayonnaise

1 teaspoon Dijon mustard

½ teaspoon Frank's Red Hot Sauce

Smoked or sweet paprika for dusting (optional)

MAKES 24 deviled eggs

Remember making deviled eggs as a kid? They were always good, but the addition of bacon makes them that much better. The hot sauce gives them a nice burst of spice.

1 Preheat the oven to 350°F.

2 Lay the bacon on a baking sheet (with sides) and bake for 10 to 13 minutes, until crisp. Blot the bacon on paper towels to remove extra grease and let cool.

3 Place the eggs in a single layer in a saucepan and cover with water. Bring to a boil, then immediately remove from the heat and cover the pan. Let the eggs sit covered for 12 minutes. Dump out the hot water and run cold water over the eggs until they are cold, then peel and set aside.

4 Mince the scallion greens and place in a large bowl. Finely chop the bacon and add to the bowl.

5 Slice the eggs in half lengthwise, placing the yolks in the bowl with the scallions.

6 Mash the yolks with the back of a fork.

7 Add the salt, pepper, mayonnaise, mustard, and hot sauce to the mashed yolks and mix well.

8 Fill the egg white halves with the egg yolk mixture using a spoon or a piping bag. Dust with smoked or plain paprika, if using. Keep cold until ready to serve.

FRIED
OKRA
WITH SPICY DIPPING SAUCE

All veggies taste better when dredged and fried, right? Okra's no exception. The subtle taste of the okra pairs well with Buffalo Sauce for dipping. (See "Deep-Frying 101" on page 77 if you're a first-time fryer.)

½ teaspoon table salt

½ cup all-purpose flour

1½ cups corn flour
(if unavailable, use corn masa)

¼ cup granulated garlic

1½ teaspoons cayenne pepper

¼ cup lemon pepper

1 large egg

2 cups buttermilk

Canola oil for deep-frying

1½ pounds fresh okra
(see Note)

Buffalo Sauce (page 36)
for serving

SERVES 4 to 6

1 In a shallow bowl, combine the salt, all-purpose flour, corn flour, granulated garlic, cayenne, and lemon pepper.

2 In a separate shallow bowl, beat the egg with the buttermilk and set aside.

3 Heat about 3 inches of oil in a deep-fryer or heavy-bottomed stockpot to about 350°F.

4 Cut the okra in to ½-inch rounds, discarding the stem and skinny tip end.

5 Coat the cut okra in the egg wash, let it drain a bit, then dredge it in the flour mixture.

6 Shake off excess flour, then fry in batches for about 3 or 4 minutes, or until golden brown.

7 Serve with the Buffalo Sauce.

NOTE When preparing okra, use fresh okra, never frozen. And use it immediately to keep it from becoming slimy.

JALAPEÑO POPPERS

WITH RANCH DRESSING

4 (7-ounce) cans whole jalapeños (about 5 to 6 per can)

4 ounces cream cheese, softened

1 teaspoon chopped garlic

½ teaspoon ground dried sage

½ cup shredded Monterey Jack cheese

½ cup shredded cheddar cheese

Canola oil for deep-frying

½ cup all-purpose flour

1 large egg

⅓ cup buttermilk

1 cup plain breadcrumbs

Buttermilk Ranch Dressing (page 37) for dipping

MAKES 20 to 24 poppers

This is a staple starter and should be included in any arsenal for the home cook. Even though they're more work than other starters, the payoff is worth it. Don't forget the ranch dressing; it can soothe the heat from the jalapeños. (See "Deep-Frying 101" on page 77 if you're a first-time fryer.) You can also make this with our Pickled Jalapeños (page 44).

1   Open the cans of jalapeños and drain them. With a sharp paring knife, carefully make a slit from just below the stem of the jalapeños to the point. Using a small spoon—or even a ½ teaspoon measurer—gently scrape out and discard the seeds and membrane. Set the seeded jalapeños aside.

2   In a bowl, combine the cream cheese with the garlic, sage, and Monterey Jack and cheddar cheeses, mixing well.

3   Stuff the cheese mixture in to the jalapeños, taking care not to tear them. It's okay if the cheese is overflowing a little.

4   In a deep-fryer or heavy-bottomed stockpot, heat 4 to 5 inches of oil to 350°F.

5   While the oil is heating, coat the peppers. Place the flour in a shallow bowl. In another shallow bowl, beat the egg with the buttermilk. Place the breadcrumbs in a third bowl. Working in batches, coat the jalapeños in the flour, shaking off the excess, then dip in the egg mixture and then dredge in the breadcrumbs.

6   When all of the jalapeños are coated and the oil is ready, begin frying in batches. Fry each for 3 to 4 minutes, until golden. Using the deep-fryer's wire basket, a slotted spoon, or a spider, remove to paper towels to absorb extra oil or drain on a wire rack.

7   Serve with Buttermilk Ranch Dressing.

SMOKY GRILLED
SHRIMP COCKTAIL
WITH SPICY GUACAMOLE

Served with our spicy guacamole, this grilled shrimp cocktail is bursting with flavor. The orange in our guac adds some sweet to the shrimp—something that you don't normally get from a cocktail sauce—and the smoky heat from the chipotle brings an unexpected additional layer of flavor.

1 **Prepare the marinade:** Combine the zests, garlic, salt, pepper, and oil in a large bowl. Add the shrimp to the bowl, toss to coat with the marinade, cover, and refrigerate for about 2 hours.

2 **Grill the shrimp:** Preheat your grill to medium heat and make a packet of presoaked wood chips in aluminum foil. Poke holes in the packet. When the grill is fully hot, place the wood chip packet on the hot coals and oil the hot grates.

3 Grill the shrimp until they are opaque, 6 to 8 minutes, depending on the size of your shrimp. Remove the shrimp from the grill and set aside to cool to room temperature.

4 **While the shrimp are cooling, make the guacamole:** Give the orange segments a quick chop to make small chunks. Set aside.

5 Peel the avocados and remove the pits. Place the avocado flesh in a bowl and, with the bottom of a small whisk or a potato masher, smash the avocados until you have a chunky pulp.

6 Add the chopped orange and the remaining ingredients to the bowl with the avocados; mix to combine. You can add more jalapeño and Chipotle Puree if you want more of a kick. Serve with the shrimp.

FOR THE MARINADE:

Zest of lime (reserve fruit for guacamole)

Zest of 1 lemon

Zest of 1 orange (reserve fruit for guacamole)

3 garlic cloves, peeled

1 teaspoon kosher salt

¼ teaspoon black pepper

2 tablespoons olive oil

★

1½ pounds jumbo or colossal shrimp, peeled and deveined

FOR THE SPICY GUACAMOLE:

1 orange (from the orange zested above), peeled and cut into segments

3 avocados

2 scallions, thinly sliced

2 tablespoons minced jalapeño, or to taste

¼ cup roughly chopped cilantro

Juice of 1 lime (from the lime zested above)

1½ teaspoons Chipotle Puree (page 32), or to taste

1½ teaspoons kosher salt

SERVES 4 to 6

POPCORN
SHRIMP
WITH CAJUN MAYO

¼ cup all-purpose flour

¾ cup corn flour (if unavailable, use corn masa)

2 tablespoons granulated garlic

¾ teaspoon cayenne pepper

2 tablespoons lemon pepper

¼ teaspoon fine salt

1 large egg

½ cup buttermilk

Canola oil for deep-frying

1½ pounds small shrimp, peeled (see Note)

Cajun Mayonnaise (page 39) for serving

Lemon wedges for serving

SERVES 4 to 6

Quick and easy to make, popcorn shrimp are always a people pleaser. Who doesn't love shoving tons of mini fried shrimp in their mouth while downing cold beers? (See "Deep-Frying 101" on page 77 if you're a first-time fryer.)

1 Combine the all-purpose flour, corn flour, granulated garlic, cayenne, lemon pepper, and salt in a shallow bowl.

2 In another shallow bowl, beat the egg with the buttermilk.

3 Heat about 3 inches of oil in a deep-fryer or heavy-bottomed stockpot to 350°F.

4 Coat the shrimp in the egg wash and let drain a bit, then dredge it in the flour mixture.

5 Shake off excess flour. Fry in batches until golden brown, 4 to 5 minutes. Using the deep-fryer's wire basket, a slotted spoon, or a spider, remove to paper towels to absorb extra oil or drain on a wire rack.

6 Serve with the Cajun Mayonnaise and lemon wedges.

NOTE The shrimp we use to make popcorn shrimp are 71 to 90 count. If you cannot find this size, "salad" or "miniature" shrimp, about 100 count, will work. Because these shrimp are so small, they do not need to be deveined.

CORNMEAL-CRUSTED

CATFISH
NUGGETS

WITH ROASTED TOMATO TARTAR SAUCE

We're talking cornmeal-coated fried fish here, so it will always delight mouths. (See "Deep-Frying 101" on page 77 if you're a first-time fryer.) This tartar sauce is easy to make, but remember to leave time for slow-roasting the tomatoes.

1 Cut the catfish into 1½- to 2-inch "bites" and set aside.

2 In a heavy-bottomed 8-inch round pot, heat 3 to 4 inches of oil (replenish if the level drops in between batches) to 350°F.

3 While the oil is heating, set up the breading bowls. Place the all-purpose flour in a shallow bowl. In another shallow bowl, beat the eggs with the milk. Combine the cornmeal, pepper, salt, and granulated garlic in a third shallow bowl.

4 Set the bowls from left to right: flour, egg mixture, and seasoned cornmeal. In batches, dredge the fish first in the flour—shaking off excess—then in the egg, then in the cornmeal, making sure it is well coated.

5 Fry the nuggets, in batches, for about 6 minutes, until they are golden. Don't overcrowd the oil. Using the deep-fryer's wire basket, a slotted spoon, or a spider, remove the fish to paper towels to absorb extra oil or drain on a wire rack.

6 Serve with the Roasted Tomato Tartar sauce.

1½ to 2 pounds skinless catfish fillets

About 3 cups canola oil for deep-frying

½ cup all-purpose flour

1 cup cornmeal

½ teaspoon ground black pepper

½ teaspoon salt

½ teaspoon granulated garlic

2 large eggs

¼ cup milk

Roasted Tomato Tartar Sauce (page 38) for serving

MAKES 24 to 30 nuggets

MARINATED & GRILLED

PORTOBELLO SKEWERS

WITH BLUE CHEESE DRESSING

FOR THE MARINADE:

1 tablespoon chopped garlic

1 teaspoon chopped fresh oregano

1 teaspoon chopped fresh thyme

½ teaspoon kosher salt

1 tablespoon sugar

1 teaspoon ground black pepper

2 tablespoons soy sauce

½ cup olive oil

1 tablespoon balsamic vinegar

4 or 5 large portobello mushrooms

12 to 18 (6-inch) bamboo skewers, soaked in water for at least 1 hour

Blue Cheese Dressing (page 36) for serving

SERVES 6 to 10

Perfect for the non-meat-eaters, you should always have these on hand. Plus, they're grilled, so health-conscious guests will appreciate them.

1 Combine all the marinade ingredients in a large bowl.

2 Cut the portobellos into 1-inch pieces—the end amount will vary depending on the size of the mushrooms. Toss with the marinade and let sit for 10 minutes, mixing once or twice.

3 Preheat your grill to moderate to high heat.

4 Thread 3 pieces of mushroom onto each bamboo skewer.

5 Just before you're ready to cook, oil the hot grates. Grill the portobellos for 5 to 7 minutes, basting with leftover marinade and turning frequently until they begin to caramelize. Be careful not to let the skewers (or mushrooms) burn (see Tip).

6 Serve with the Blue Cheese Dressing.

> **TIP** To help prevent the skewers from burning, take a strip of aluminum foil, long enough to cover the area you will be grilling on, and double it over. Lay it on the grill. When you place the skewers on the grill, make sure that the exposed skewer rests on the foil while the mushrooms are on the grill.

SPICED
PECANS

These sweet and spicy pecans are addictive. They serve double duty as an ingredient in The Wright Salad (page 108), and they're a great way to satisfy the hungry masses while your grill fires up.

2 cups pecan halves

½ teaspoon smoked paprika

1½ teaspoons chili powder

½ teaspoon ground cumin

½ teaspoon ground coriander

½ teaspoon ground black pepper

½ teaspoon kosher salt

½ teaspoon sugar

1½ tablespoons olive oil

MAKES 2 cups

1 Toss the pecans with the smoked paprika, chili powder, cumin, coriander, pepper, salt, and sugar. Add the oil and toss to coat evenly and let sit for 30 minutes.

2 Meanwhile, preheat the oven to 325°F.

3 Spread the pecans on a baking sheet and bake for 15 minutes. Don't turn them.

4 Cool before using or storing. They'll keep in an airtight container for several weeks.

COMPLETELY SUPERFLUOUS FINAL FOUR DRINKING GAMES:

WHEN I WATCH any sporting event, I like to engage in random and silly drinking games with my pals. The Final Four is no different. (By the by, if you're wondering who I root for, it's always Bacone College in Muskogee, Oklahoma.) Here's a quick list of my top drinking cues during the March craziness:

• Take a sip after every ten points.

• Drink every time Dick Vitale screams erroneously.

• Drink every time Dick Vitale screams appropriately.

• Imbibe whenever the cheerleading troupe tosses someone into the air.

• Make it a double gulp if they drop the poor girl on the landing.

• Down a shot whenever you see a coach mouthing swear words.

SOUPS, STEWS

&

STURDY SALADS

ON MOST DAYS, MARCH

IS STILL SOUP-AND-STEW WEATHER UP NORTH AND IT'S

also the time of one of the greatest parties at Brother Jimmy's—St. Patty's Day. In fact, looking around the packed room at the original Brother Jimmy's location on Saint Patrick's Day is enough to make you wonder if anyone still works on this holiday dedicated to booze. By 2:30 in the afternoon, the annual parade has wound its way North through Manhattan, ceasing just a stone's throw from our Upper East Side Second Avenue location, where we first opened. With the culmination of the festivities so close by, legions of firemen, police officers, loyal Irishmen, and party animals alike are left wandering around the area looking for a place to continue the revelry. Luckily, they always find us.

In through our door they stream. Hundreds and hundreds of uniformed men, all decked out in their finest dress blues, their hats slightly askew, their ties slackened, and their pristine white gloves stuffed underneath their epaulets. "I don't want to get green beer on 'em," one fireman with a thick Brooklyn accent shouts to his brigade member, who nods in agreement. Company patches on the blazers of these dedicated men read like a map of the world. FDNY, Yonkers, New Mexico, even from Cork, Ireland. All crammed into Brother Jimmy's so close they can barely free an elbow to get that frosty beer to their mouths.

Even though we're not an Irish bar, those in the know flock to Brother Jimmy's on St. Patty's day because fun awaits them inside. One hundred cases of green-canned, shamrock-adorned Bud Lights are there chilling in our coolers. Forty cases of Jameson whiskey are in there waiting to be poured onto trays of shot glasses and passed 'round. Bubbly waitresses in green and white fluffy hats, rocking "Kiss me, I'm Irish" shirts, are there. Men in kilts, toting bagpipes and drums are there, itching for a request to play. Girls who flash the firemen and cops their prettiest smile (and sometimes other parts of their bodies) while trying to steal a hat, or badge, or gloves are in there, working their charms. Newsboy caps, green balloons, green beer, Irish Car Bombs, more plaid than you can imagine, and the instantly recognizable strains of Dropkick Murphys and U2 are all in there, combining perfectly to make it a memorable party.

We're thrilled at the almost tangible feeling of love and camaraderie in a Brother Jimmy's, which only heightens on St. Patrick's Day. It's like stepping into a pub in Dublin; everyone has their arms around one another, singing and belting out the lyrics to their favorite Irish ditty. Glasses

clink, smiles abound, and the energy in the room can't be topped. Girls who need help getting a drink are given a lift—literally—by any fireman with a keen eye. You'll catch them tossing lovely lasses over a shoulder, rescue-style, and marching up to the bar, all the while laughing.

Our food is the centerpiece of the party. Buckets of tangy wings, mounds of crispy fried chicken, and heaps of slow-smoked brisket are flying out of the kitchen to eager stomachs' delight. All the dishes Brother Jimmy's patrons have come to adore are served up hot and fresh, providing the perfect base for any stomach that's about to embark on a tour de force of drinking. Also turning up on tables are our filling soups and stews.

It's the ideal time of year for them. St. Patty's Day signifies the real end of winter and the beginning of spring (sorry, Punxsutawney Phil). The days are starting to get longer, the temperature is starting to rise, but there's still a hint of winter in the air. We like to cut through the chill with a warm bowl of nourishment. The Irish may not be renowned for their food, but they did get soups and stews right: Toss a whole bunch of ingredients—each tasty enough on their own merits—into a boiling pot, let simmer and reduce, and ladle out.

These aren't wimpy, brothy concoctions that are so thin you can drink them through a straw; these are hearty meals in their own right. Something you'd find simmering atop a stove in the barracks of our aforementioned firefighting friends. But you don't have to be a bona fide smoke eater to enjoy our Smoky BBQ Chili—though you may need the boys in blue to calm the fire in your mouth, depending on how spicy you like it.

Since soups and stews are very comforting foods, they're also optimal for the day after you've spent punishing your liver with liquor and are battling a formidable hangover. Roll out of bed, swear aloud you'll never have that many whiskey shots ever again, squint at our recipes, chop everything up, dump it all in a large pot, and return to the couch for a marathon of bad television while it cooks. Shout to your roommate/family member/loved one/dog to give it a good stir every now and again, and you're well on your way to a tasty hangover cure.

THESE AREN'T WIMPY, BROTHY CONCOCTIONS THAT ARE SO THIN YOU CAN DRINK THEM through a straw; these are hearty meals . . .

We'll show you how we do Brunswick Stew, traditionally made of scraps, roadkill, and generally whatever else was handy in Southern kitchens of yesteryear. Don't worry about needing flattened raccoon for ours; we've opted for smoked pork and shredded chicken, corn, and BBQ sauce. Feel free to step up the heat, of course, by upping the chili ante in the dishes, but perhaps not so much that you suddenly remember that questionable hook-up from the night before.

And because March is the time when Northerners get a glimmer of spring to come, salads become appealing once again. We included a few, in case you feel you need something green on St. Patty's Day besides green beer, or at least on other days of the year.

All you'll need to do is invite your pals—and possibly some firemen and cops. (If you do find yourself in the company of your city's bravest and finest, make sure you don't steal pieces of their uniforms; they get docked personal days for missing badges and caps.) Whatever you do, don't call in sick to work the day after St. Patty's Day. Or, if you do end up being *that* guy, just don't blame us. We didn't force that sixth Car Bomb down your throat.

PLAYLIST

Although you don't have to keep it all in the Irish musical genre, here are some of our favorite ditties from across the pond. Mixed in we have some standards that everyone likes to drink to. So ready your Guinness, chill your Jameson, and get the party started with these songs.

WILLIE NELSON
I GOTTA GET DRUNK

THE POGUES
TUESDAY MORNING

U2
SUNDAY BLOODY SUNDAY

DROPKICK MURPHYS
HEROES FROM OUR PAST

FLOGGING MOLLY
DEVIL'S DANCE FLOOR

THE CHIEFTAINS
O'SULLIVAN'S MARCH

THE CLANCY BROTHERS
TIM FINNEGAN'S WAKE

GAELIC STORM
AN IRISH PARTY

THE SAW DOCTORS
I USETA LOVER

U2
PRIDE (IN THE NAME OF LOVE)

ELVIS COSTELLO
I CAN'T STAND UP FOR FALLING DOWN

THE MIGHTY MIGHTY BOSSTONES
THE IMPRESSION THAT I GET

ELVIS COSTELLO
CLUBLAND

THE SAW DOCTORS
HAY WRAP

FLOGGING MOLLY
WHAT'S LEFT OF THE FLAG

THE SAW DOCTORS
N17

GAELIC STORM
CECILIA

DROPKICK MURPHYS
I'M SHIPPING UP TO BOSTON

U2
BEAUTIFUL DAY

BRUNSWICK STEW

Although traditionally this was made with whatever meat was available (including roadkill), we use leftover smoked pork butt and chicken. You can make it with fresh ingredients, but you can use leftovers, too. You can still go ahead and include possum, if you're particularly daring. And a bad driver.

1 Melt the butter in a large pot or Dutch oven over medium-low heat and add the onion and garlic. Cook for 4 to 5 minutes, until the onions start to soften. Be careful not to burn the garlic.

2 Cut the corn kernels off the cobs. Add to the onions, along with remaining ingredients. Bring to a simmer and cook for about 25 minutes.

1 tablespoon unsalted butter

1 cup chopped Spanish onion

1 tablespoon chopped garlic

2 ears corn

3 tablespoons Brother Jimmy's Original BBQ Sauce (page 31)

1 teaspoon Worcestershire sauce

1 teaspoon Frank's Red Hot Sauce

1 (28-ounce) can diced tomatoes

4 cups chicken stock (store-bought is fine)

2½ cups leftover cooked pork, cut into ¾-inch cubes

1¾ cups pulled leftover cooked chicken (leg and thigh)

MAKES 4 to 6 servings

DRINKS: IF THERE'S ONE THING THE IRISH KNOW, it's how to drink. Just try telling a true Irishman that the bar is closed and, just like MacGyver, he'll figure out a way to get some liquor in your system. As a result of years of practice, our neighbors from across the pond have whipped up some tasty concoctions that are perfectly suited to St. Patrick's Day (though there's no need to limit these libations to merely one day of the year). See pages 64–65 for a variety of St. Patty's Day drinks.

BEEF & PUMPKIN STEW
WITH PINTO BEANS

2½ to 3 pounds chuck roast, trimmed of excess fat and cut into 1½-inch pieces

Salt and ground black pepper

½ cup all-purpose flour

¼ cup olive oil

1½ cups chopped red onion

1 cup chopped carrot

6 garlic cloves, roughly chopped

1 teaspoon ancho chile powder

2 tablespoons tomato paste

1 pound dry pinto beans, soaked overnight (see Note, page 99)

1 small sugar pumpkin or medium winter squash, such as butternut, peeled, seeded, and cut into large chunks

3 poblano chiles, roasted, peeled, seeded, and diced (see page 108)

3 teaspoons salt, plus more if needed

4 to 5 cups chicken or beef stock (store-bought is fine)

SERVES 6

This is a hearty stew that we like to prepare when the first sugar pumpkins appear at our local farmers' market. It has the "it's time to hunker down for winter" feel to it. It's really fall in a bowl.

1 Season the beef with salt and pepper and toss in the flour to coat, shaking off the excess.

2 In a heavy-bottomed pot with a lid or a Dutch oven, heat the oil over medium-high heat and brown the meat in batches, a few minutes per side.

3 Remove the meat from the pot and add the onions, carrots, and garlic; reduce the heat to medium and cook for about 5 minutes, until the vegetables begin to soften.

4 Add the ancho chile powder, then the tomato paste, and stir to coat the vegetables.

5 Drain the beans and add them to the pot, along with the pumpkin, poblanos, 3 teaspoons of salt, and the stock.

6 Increase the heat to medium-high, bring the stew to a boil, then reduce the heat to low and cover the pot. Cook for about 2 hours, until the beef is very tender. Taste and add more salt if necessary.

SMOKY
BBQ CHILI

1½ pounds ground beef

2 cups diced Spanish onion

2 cups diced green pepper

1½ teaspoons chopped garlic

1 jalapeño, finely chopped

1 tablespoon ground cumin

1 tablespoon ground coriander

½ teaspoon ancho chile powder

½ teaspoon chipotle chile powder

1½ teaspoons dried oregano

1½ teaspoons kosher salt

1 (32-ounce) can crushed tomatoes

1 (15-ounce) can diced tomatoes with their juice

2 (15-ounce) cans dark red kidney beans, drained and rinsed

1 bottle beer (we use an amber ale)

SERVES 6

Chili is good for when you're hungover. Smoke some beef, toss everything in a pot, and lie down while your brain pain subsides. Chili is one of those things that can be eaten year round, so don't feel the need to stick to wintertime for making this classic.

1 Prepare your smoker or grill for barbecuing, using the indirect heat setup (see page 15), and preheat to 240°F.

2 In a heavy-bottomed pot or Dutch oven over medium-high heat, brown the beef with the onion, green pepper, garlic, and jalapeño, stirring to break up any lumps.

3 Place in a baking dish and smoke for 1½ hours.

4 Transfer the meat back to the pot or Dutch oven and add the cumin, coriander, ancho chile powder, chipotle chile powder, oregano, salt, crushed and diced tomatoes, beans, and beer.

5 Place over medium heat and bring to a simmer; reduce the heat and cook for about 90 minutes to develop the flavors, stirring often to prevent burning.

RED BEANS & RICE

The Brother Jimmy's version of a New Orleans tradition. After the prep work, everything marries on its own in the pot, to a delicious finish.

1 Drain and rinse the beans; set them aside.

2 Heat the oil in a heavy-bottomed pot or Dutch oven over low heat; add the sausage and cook until browned.

3 Add the onion, celery, green pepper, and garlic and cook until the vegetables are softened, about 5 minutes.

4 Add the remaining ingredients, including the beans, increase the heat to medium-high, and bring to a boil. Reduce the heat and simmer for 1½ to 2 hours, until the beans are tender and the mixture is thick.

5 Remove the bunch of thyme, and serve the beans over your favorite white rice.

> NOTE For quick soaking, place the beans in a pot and cover with double the amount of water. Bring to a boil, then immediately remove from the heat and let sit for 1 hour.

1 pound dry red kidney beans, soaked overnight (see Note)

3 tablespoons olive oil

1 andouille sausage link (about 1 pound), sliced

2 cups diced Spanish onion

¾ cup diced celery

1 cup diced green pepper

2 tablespoons chopped garlic

7 cups water or stock (store-bought is fine)

2 bay leaves

½ teaspoon cayenne pepper

¼ teaspoon ground dried sage

1 teaspoon Worcestershire sauce

1 teaspoon Frank's Red Hot Sauce

1 cup tomato puree

Small bunch fresh thyme, tied up with butcher's twine

Cooked white rice, for serving

SERVES 8 to 10

SPLIT PEA SOUP
WITH HAM HOCK

1 tablespoon olive oil

3 garlic cloves, chopped

1½ cups diced Spanish onion

1 cup diced celery

1 cup diced carrot

1 ham hock

1 pound split peas

1 bay leaf

2 or 3 sprigs fresh thyme

½ teaspoon ground coriander

½ teaspoon ground cumin

10 cups water or chicken stock
(store-bought stock is fine)

1 teaspoon kosher salt,
plus more if needed

½ teaspoon ground black
pepper, plus more if needed

SERVES 6 to 8

It's a good soup, and the ham only heightens the flavor of the bowl. Feel free to toss some croutons on top for an added crunch.

1 Heat the oil in a heavy-bottomed pot or Dutch oven over medium heat. Add the garlic, onion, celery, and carrot and sauté until the vegetables start to soften, about 5 minutes.

2 Add the ham hock, split peas, bay leaf, thyme, coriander, cumin, and water or stock. Increase the heat to medium-high, bring to a boil, then reduce the heat and simmer for about 1 hour (or longer depending on the age of the peas), until the split peas are tender and broken.

3 Turn off the heat, remove the ham hock, and set to cool until you can handle it (5 minutes in the freezer works well).

4 Remove the meat from the ham hock, discarding the fat, skin, and bone. Chop the meat and add it to the soup, along with the salt and pepper.

5 Give the soup a good stir, taste, and adjust the seasoning if necessary.

6 If you'd like a very smooth soup, run it through the blender, in batches, taking care not to burn yourself.

SUMMER
GAZPACHO

This is the quintessential summer soup because it's served cold. It's best made when the tomatoes and peppers are all at their peak. It's cool and refreshing, and you can add some chilled grilled shrimp to make it more of a meal. Or it can double as a shot with a raw oyster.

1 Dice all the vegetables and place them in a large bowl. Add the remaining ingredients, cover, and refrigerate to marinate for a couple of hours.

2 Blend the vegetables and liquid in batches until the soup is relatively smooth.

3 Adjust the seasoning to your liking and serve cold.

2 pounds vine-ripened tomatoes (about 3 large)

1 red pepper, cut in half, seeds and membranes removed

1 green pepper, cut in half, seeds and membranes removed

½ red onion

1 seedless cucumber (also called hothouse or English cucumber)

¾ cup packed flat-leaf Italian parsley

1½ teaspoons kosher salt, plus more if needed

2 garlic cloves, smashed

¼ cup good-quality red wine vinegar

¼ cup extra-virgin olive oil

½ teaspoon ground black pepper

1 tablespoon Frank's Red Hot Sauce

1 cup tomato juice

SERVES 6 to 8

ICE BOWL: FOR EXTRA BONUS POINTS, spice up the gazpacho's presentation by serving it in bowls made from ice. Although they do sell molds for exactly this, you can save some cash and shopping time by making them at home. They're so simple to craft, I make them for my guests around the farm. Simply take two bowls—one that fits inside another and is lighter—with about a half inch of distance in between, and add water to the bottom bowl. Toss in something heavy to make the floating bowl sink a smidgen, but not so far down it touches the bottom bowl. Then pop in the freezer. To remove the inner bowl, run under hot water until it loosens. These ice bowls always get rave reviews.

SHRIMP & ANDOUILLE
GUMBO

½ cup vegetable oil

¾ cup all-purpose flour

3 cups diced Spanish onion

3 cups diced green pepper

1 cup diced celery

1 pound andouille sausage, cut in half lengthwise and sliced into ¼-inch half-moons

8 cups chicken stock (store-bought is fine)

1½ teaspoons fresh thyme

2 bay leaves

1 teaspoon cayenne pepper, or to taste

1 to 1½ teaspoons salt

½ teaspoon ground black pepper

3 cups okra, cut into ¾-inch slices

1 pound medium to large shrimp, peeled and deveined

Cooked white rice, for serving

SERVES 8

A little bit of land and a little bit of sea happily combine in the pot to create a sweet and spicy gumbo, perfect for any meal, anytime.

1 Heat the oil in a heavy-bottomed pot or Dutch oven over medium-high heat. Add the flour and cook, whisking constantly, until the roux turns a deep brown, 10 to 15 minutes.

2 Reduce the heat and add the onion, green pepper, and celery. Cook, stirring constantly, for about 5 minutes, then add the sausage and cook for about 3 minutes, until it starts to brown a bit.

3 Add the stock in small amounts, stirring well after each addition to break up the roux and make a smooth gumbo.

4 Add the thyme, bay leaves, cayenne, salt, and pepper. Bring to a boil, then reduce the heat and simmer for 20 minutes.

5 Add the okra and simmer for 40 minutes more, until the gumbo has thickened.

6 Add the shrimp. Cook for 8 minutes, until the shrimp is cooked.

7 Serve over your favorite cooked white rice recipe.

SMOKY CORN SOUP

This recipe was conceived when customers started asking for some "lighter" starters. You'd never know from the velvety texture that this soup has no dairy.

1 **Make the stock:** Remove the kernels from the ears. Reserve the kernels for the soup and toss the cobs into a stockpot. Roughly chop all the stock vegetables and toss them, along with the remaining ingredients, into the stockpot. Simmer over medium heat, for about 1 hour, until reduced by almost half. Strain, discard the vegetables and corn cobs, and use the resulting stock to make the soup.

2 **Make the soup:** Heat the oil in a heavy-bottomed pot or Dutch oven over low heat. Add the smoked onion, garlic, and celery and sauté until they soften, about 5 minutes.

3 Add the remaining ingredients, increase the heat to medium-high, bring to a simmer, then reduce the heat and simmer for about 45 minutes, until the vegetables are very soft. Remove the thyme branches and bay leaf.

4 Puree the soup in batches in a blender and pass through a strainer—this gets out all the tough parts of the corn kernel and leaves you with a velvety smooth soup.

FOR THE CORN STOCK:

8 ears corn

3 medium Yukon Gold potatoes

3 stalks celery

1 large red onion

2 carrots

6 whole black peppercorns

1 bay leaf

4 garlic cloves

2 or 3 sprigs fresh thyme

16 cups water

FOR THE SOUP:

2 tablespoons olive oil

2 cups diced Spanish onion, smoked over indirect heat for 1 hour

1 tablespoon chopped garlic

2 stalks celery, thinly sliced

Corn kernels from the cobs (reserved from the stock)

8 cups corn stock (from above)

1½ cups diced Yukon Gold potatoes

1½ teaspoons kosher salt

½ teaspoon ground black pepper

2 or 3 sprigs fresh thyme

1 bay leaf

SERVES 6 to 8

BACON, POTATO & CHEDDAR SOUP

2 pounds Yukon Gold potatoes (5 to 6 large)

8 slices applewood-smoked bacon (or any other smoky bacon)

2 cups diced Spanish onion

4 garlic cloves, crushed

5 cups water or chicken stock (store-bought stock is fine)

1 cup milk

1 bay leaf

3 cups grated sharp cheddar cheese

1 teaspoon salt, plus more if needed

½ teaspoon ground black pepper, plus more if needed

SERVES 6 to 8

This will keep everyone hovering around the stove for a taste, as it has all the ingredients people love. Don't be afraid to add more bacon. Or extra cheese—just think of it as a cheese blanket keeping your soup toasty.

1 Peel the potatoes and cut them into chunks. Hold them in a bowl of cold water until ready to use to prevent discoloration.

2 Cut the bacon into 1-inch pieces. Heat a heavy-bottomed pot or Dutch oven over medium-low heat and add the bacon. Cook the bacon slowly. When it starts to crisp around the edges, add the onion and garlic and cook until softened, about 5 minutes.

3 Add the potatoes, water or stock, milk, and bay leaf. Bring to a boil, then lower the heat and simmer for about 45 minutes, until the potatoes are very soft.

4 Stir in the cheese, salt, and pepper. Remove the bay leaf. In small batches, puree the soup in a blender, transferring the finished soup into another pot or serving vessel. Remember, this is very hot liquid you are working with, so be careful. Put a dishtowel over the cover of the blender in case any hot liquid tries to jump out. Never fill the blender more than half full. Do not overblend, or the potatoes might become gummy.

5 Taste and adjust the seasoning if needed.

SWEET POTATO
CHIPOTLE SOUP

With sweet and spicy notes abounding, this satisfying soup is great for lunch, or in a larger bowl for dinner. It pairs nicely with the Marinated and Grilled Portobello Skewers (page 88), and you can serve it chilled in the summertime.

1 In a heavy-bottomed pot or Dutch oven, heat the oil over medium heat. Add the onion and garlic and sauté until softened, about 5 minutes. Add the celery, carrot, sweet potato, thyme, and water or stock.

2 Bring to a boil, then reduce the heat and simmer for about 45 minutes, until the vegetables soften.

3 Add the chipotle puree and salt.

4 In batches, puree the soup in a blender (don't fill the blender more than half full). Use a kitchen towel to hold the lid, as hot liquids can be explosive. Adjust the seasoning if necessary.

3 tablespoons olive oil

1 cup diced Spanish onion

4 garlic cloves, chopped

2 stalks celery, diced

1 large carrot, diced

1½ pounds sweet potatoes (about 2 large), diced

3 sprigs fresh thyme

8 cups water or stock (store-bought stock is fine)

2 teaspoons Chipotle Puree (page 32)

1½ teaspoons salt, plus more if needed

SERVES 6 to 8

GAMES: MY PEN PALS AND I like to play these games every St. Patty's Day. They're simple to play and always fun. Just don't invite my neighbor, Bay Connor—that swine always cheats.

DONKEY BOLLOCKS

Spread a deck of cards facedown around an empty glass and have each player pour in a bit of their drink. This is the "donkey's bollocks." Each player takes a turn pulling a card and guessing if it is red or black. If correct, he balances the card on the glass. If not, he must drink, then put his card on the glass. If any player knocks the pile over, he must drink the donkey's bollocks. Nice people will pour the same beverage in the glass. Cruel jerks won't.

IRISH QUARTERS

The lead player fills a cup with however much beer he wishes. Bear in mind however much beer you put in, you'll be drinking very shortly.

The lead player spins a quarter and tries to drink the beer as quickly as possible. If a player can successfully down his beer, replenish the cup for the next person, and pick up the quarter before it stops spinning, the game moves onto the next player. If not, that player is forced to try again with a fresh cup until he is successful or unable to continue. The latter would be because he is absolutely hammered.

BREAKOUT RECIPES

STURDY SALADS

We understand that not a lot of salad greens are being eaten with Southern food. Salad's just not a typical menu item. But Brother Jimmy's has a fix for that with The Wright Salad, Brother Jimmy's Wedge with Fried Onions, Southern Salad, and Buffalo Fried Chicken Cobb Salad. These aren't your average little fluffy salads. These are hearty and filling. And they have a number of components that can be prepped ahead of time. It's our attempt to get a little roughage in your diet, because a steady stream of barbecue and fried goodness isn't going to keep you alive and kicking for long. We're kidding. But not really. Eat your vegetables. Your mother would be pleased.

BUFFALO FRIED CHICKEN COBB SALAD

Buffalo Chicken Breasts (page 160), cooled

8 slices applewood-smoked bacon
(or any other smoky bacon)

½ head iceberg lettuce, cut up

½ head romaine lettuce, cut up

1 large ripe tomato, diced

⅔ cup minced red onion

3 avocados, peeled, pitted, and diced

⅔ cup crumbled blue cheese

1½ cups Blue Cheese Dressing (page 36),
or your dressing of choice

1 Preheat the oven to 350°F. Lay the bacon on a sheet pan and bake for 10 to 13 minutes, until crisp. Blot on paper towels to remove extra grease, let cool, then crumble.

2 In a large salad bowl, toss all the ingredients except the dressing together, then toss with the dressing and plate up.

SERVES 6

BROTHER JIMMY'S WEDGE WITH FRIED ONIONS

6 slices applewood-smoked bacon
(or any other smoky bacon)

¾ cup all-purpose flour

2¼ teaspoons paprika

½ teaspoon cayenne pepper

¾ teaspoon granulated garlic

½ teaspoon ground white pepper

1 teaspoon salt

About 4 cups canola oil for deep-frying

1 Spanish onion, sliced into paper-thin rounds

1 head iceberg lettuce

1½ cups Blue Cheese Dressing (page 36)

1 large ripe tomato, cut into small chunks

. . . .

1 Preheat the oven to 350°F.

2 Lay the bacon on a sheet pan, place in the oven, and bake for 10 to 13 minutes, until crisp. Blot on paper towels to remove extra grease, cool, and cut into ½-inch pieces.

3 In a shallow bowl, combine the flour with the paprika, cayenne, granulated garlic, white pepper, and salt and set aside.

4 Heat 4 to 5 inches of oil in a deep-fryer or heavy-bottomed stockpot to 350°F. Toss the onion rounds with the spiced flour, shake off the excess flour, and fry in batches until crisp, about 2 to 4 minutes. Using a wire basket, slotted spoon, or a spider, remove the fried onions to paper towels to absorb extra oil or drain on a wire rack.

5 Remove any wilted leaves from the lettuce. Holding the lettuce in two hands, firmly hit the stem end on the table. This should make it easy to pull out the core. Next, cut the head into 6 wedges.

6 Place each wedge on a plate and pour the Blue Cheese Dressing over them. Divide the tomato and bacon among the plates.

7 Top each wedge with some of the fried onions.

SERVES 6

SOUTHERN SALAD

18 extra-large shrimp, peeled and deveined

2 tablespoons olive oil

Salt and ground black pepper

12 ounces andouille sausage

½ head romaine lettuce, cut up

½ head iceberg lettuce, cut up

1 large ripe tomato, cut into wedges

½ cup minced red onion

1 cup shredded cheddar cheese

¾ cup Herb Vinaigrette (page 108),
or another favorite dressing

½ recipe Blackened Chicken (page 181), diced

. . . .

1 Preheat the grill to medium-high. In a large bowl, toss the shrimp with the oil and season with salt and pepper. Place the shrimp on the grill for 3 to 5 minutes on each side, until they look opaque and start to curl up.

2 Cut the sausage into long diagonal slices, about 3 inches long and ¼ inch thick. Cook on the grill for 2 minutes per side, turning to leave grill marks.

3 In a large bowl, toss the lettuces, tomato, and onion with the cheese, then toss with the Herb Vinaigrette and place on a serving platter or in a large shallow bowl.

4 Arrange the shrimp, sausage, and chicken on top and serve.

SERVES 6

THE WRIGHT SALAD

FOR THE HERB VINAIGRETTE:

1½ teaspoons chopped flat-leaf Italian parsley

1½ teaspoons chopped fresh thyme

5 tablespoons red wine vinegar

¾ teaspoon kosher salt

¼ teaspoon ground black pepper

¾ cup extra-virgin olive oil

MAKES about 1 cup

FOR THE SALAD:

¾ cup wild rice

4 cups water

2 teaspoons salt

1 large sweet potato, cut into ½-inch cubes

1 tablespoon olive oil

1 poblano chile

1 apple (we prefer Granny Smith)

½ lemon

1 head romaine lettuce

¾ cup dried cherries

¾ cup very thinly sliced sweet onion (such as Vidalia)

½ cup Herb Vinaigrette, or as needed

¾ cup Spiced Pecans (page 89)

SERVES 4 to 6

1 **Make the herb vinaigrette:** In a bowl, combine all the ingredients except the oil. Slowly whisk in the oil to incorporate. Set aside.

2 **Make the salad:** Place the wild rice in a large saucepan with the water and salt. Bring to a boil, then reduce the heat, cover, and simmer for 45 to 50 minutes, until tender. Drain any excess water, cool to room temperature, and set aside.

3 Meanwhile, preheat the oven to 350°F. In a large bowl, toss the sweet potatoes with the oil and place on a baking sheet. Roast for 20 to 25 minutes, or until tender and lightly colored. Remove from the oven, cool to room temperature, and set aside.

4 Roast the poblano, ideally by placing it over an open flame—a hot grill or a gas burner on your home stove works well—or by placing it underneath the broiler, getting it as close to the heat as you can. Turn it frequently until the skin chars and starts to blister. Place the poblano in a small bowl and cover with plastic wrap. Let rest for 10 to 15 minutes. When the poblano is cool enough to handle, peel off all the charred skin and remove the seeds. Cut into ½-inch squares.

5 While the poblano is resting, peel the apple and cut it into ½-inch cubes. To prevent discoloration, place the cubes in a bowl and cover with water. Squeeze in the ½ lemon, let sit for 5 minutes, and drain. Cut the lettuce into ribbons, place in a large salad bowl, add the wild rice, sweet potato, poblano, apple, dried cherries, onions, and Spiced Pecans, and toss. Add ½ cup of the Herb Vinaigrette or more, if desired, and toss to coat.

PORK

WE HAVE A COMBO

ON THE BROTHER JIMMY'S MENU NAMED JIMMY'S PIG PICK,

which allows guests to select four or five different types of dishes. Occasionally diners will inquire as to the name, giving us the chance to explain a little Southern tradition called pig pickin' that has been making backyards tasty hangouts for hundreds of years.

Otherwise known as a pig roast, the event revolves around a large group of people coming together to literally pick away at a roasted hog. As for where this lovely activity evolved from, the contemporary version was born when churches and large communities would hold pig pickin' feasts around the turn of the nineteenth century, when everyone would be allowed to come together for the day to enjoy pig roasts despite ongoing segregation laws.

But if you go back a little further than the 1800s, the true history of the pig roast can be traced to early Southern settlers. With food—particularly protein—scarce and fields not quite yet cultivated for farming, locals would turn pigs loose in their township's woods. Considered a low-maintenance animal that required no daily care, the hogs could forage for their own food. And given that they'll chow down just about anything, ample eats weren't much of an issue.

When the settlers spotted a particularly plump porker sauntering nearby, it was time for a hunt. Because swine have a bit of intelligence and are rather quick, the pursuit wasn't the easiest of feats and was typically a townwide event, with everyone lending a hand in trying to capture the savvy snouted beast. Once the townspeople overtook their foe, the pig was hoisted triumphantly on a pole and carried into town, where it was roasted. The resulting meal turned into a festive party to honor all the hard work that had gone into putting this fantastic meal on the table.

Thankfully, you don't have to chase down and kill your own hog to get some tantalizing pork on your plate nowadays (although if you're so inclined, Godspeed to you). So in the South, the impetus for bashes featuring a roasted pig shifted from celebrating the victory over a wild animal to celebrating a hopeful victory over an opposing sports team. We're talking about tailgating.

In Southern culture, the tailgate is as much of a part of pork barbecue culture as pigs themselves. Particularly prevalent with college sports—which in the Bible Belt are sometimes more highly regarded than religion—the tailgate rituals are extreme and the mouthwatering food that's churned out in parking lots will usually top what's being dished out at nearby established restaurants.

Southern college rivalries run deeper and more dangerously than the waters of the Mississippi River. (Remember the Alabama fan who poisoned and killed the famed 130-year-old Auburn oak tree that served as the college's unofficial mascot?) The big game is a perfect reason to break out the portable grill and some choice cuts of pork and pop open a few frosty brews. You can even put the suds in that awesome hard hat with the two cup holders and dangling straws for free-hands ability to man the sizzling grill, you party animal.

People will always join together in the common goal of beating a worthy adversary, whoever they're pitted against, be it a crafty pig or a sports team. The spirit and verve that drive the passion behind tailgating parties are the same from the pig pickin's of yesteryear. Both of which are precisely the embodiment of how our guests spend their nights at Brother Jimmy's, particularly during pregame rituals (some of our customers have come to indoctrinate them as mandatory). Whether the NCAA tourney is in full swing or there is a Florida State versus Florida football game, the pregame prep is as insane in Brother Jimmy's as if you were in the actual parking lot. We play the right music—including the collegiate fight songs—between time-outs and commercial breaks to keep the good times going.

We do such a solid job of re-creating the tailgate that our customers occasionally forget they aren't actually at the game, which is most noticeable when they're screaming at the TVs as though they're sitting right on the fifty-yard line. We'd suggest you bring earplugs should you have the pleasure of experiencing this firsthand, but sometimes the shouts are rather humorous and worth a listen. Clad to the hilt in their team's attire and jerseys under this umbrella of hospitality in this fun atmosphere, our patrons embrace the feeling of camaraderie with friends and family. They unite to eat merrily and celebrate life in our booths and tables. The main difference between a tailgate and Brother Jimmy's is that in our restaurants we've handled the cooking for you. And we'll crack your beers open.

THE SPIRIT AND VERVE THAT DRIVE THE PASSION BEHIND TAILGATING PARTIES are the same from the pig pickin's of yesteryear.

When you take your turn in the kitchen, whether you're roasting a whole hog in your backyard or dropping some ribs onto a small grill you've yanked out of your trunk in the stadium's parking lot, the resulting meals can be equally awesome with our step-by-step directions to pork domination. Our famed ribs recipes—the Northern-Style Ribs, the Dry Rub Ribs, and our Southern Rub Ribs—are included, as is our staple slow-smoked Carolina-Style Pulled Pork. And we've turned the taste dial up with the simple addition of an array of fruits to a number of the dishes, as pork pairs astoundingly well with the likes of pineapples, peaches, and oranges. We've got dishes for game days and for any occasion. We've even included some seriously drool-worthy sausage-and-ancho chile–stuffed pork chops, because what's better than pork with a hidden pocket of more pork inside?

We'll go over how to smoke and grill everything to tender perfection, no matter how large or small your cooking apparatus. The cool thing about cooking barbecue at a tailgate is that you'll have more than enough time to smoke the pork, figuring that you fire up the grill around noon for a 4 P.M. game. Just remember to pace yourself with the partying. It's going to be a long day, so try not to get so wasted during the pregaming that you're too hammered to be actually allowed into the stadium. No one likes *that* guy.

PLAYLIST

Get fired up before the big game with these high-energy rock tunes. Music can be the ultimate energizer, and these songs will be sure to get you into the mood to beat the pulp out of whichever rival you're up against. (Tip: This mix is best enjoyed when paired with an ice-cold beer, so have plenty on hand.)

THE SURFARIS
WIPE OUT

OZZY OSBOURNE
CRAZY TRAIN

VAN HALEN
JUMP

RAM JAM
BLACK BETTY

KISS
ROCK 'N ROLL ALL NIGHT

THE WHO
PINBALL WIZARD

METALLICA
ENTER SANDMAN

GREEN DAY
BASKET CASE

OK GO
HERE IT GOES AGAIN

BLINK-182
WHAT'S MY AGE AGAIN?

JIMMY EAT WORLD
THE MIDDLE

JET
ARE YOU GOING TO BE MY GIRL?

RED HOT CHILI PEPPERS
CAN'T STOP

GUNS N' ROSES
WELCOME TO THE JUNGLE

FOO FIGHTERS
BEST OF YOU

WOLFMOTHER
JOKER & THE THIEF

GOOD CHARLOTTE
LIFESTYLES OF THE RICH & FAMOUS

AC/DC
THUNDERSTRUCK

THE WHITE STRIPES
SEVEN NATION ARMY

STONE TEMPLE PILOTS
INTERSTATE LOVE SONG

NORTHERN-STYLE
RIBS

These are our most recognizable ribs because of the red sauce they're slathered in. You don't need special seasonings because the smoke and the sauce add more than enough flavor.

3 racks St. Louis–style ribs (see sidebar, below)

3 tablespoons kosher salt

3 to 4 cups Brother Jimmy's Original BBQ Sauce (page 31)

SERVE 6 to 8

1 Prepare your smoker or grill for barbecuing, using the indirect heat setup (see page 15) with a drip pan in place, and preheat to 210°F.

2 Pat the ribs dry, then season with the salt.

3 Pour some water in the drip pan and place some presoaked wood chunks or a packet of presoaked wood chips directly on the hot coals. Oil the hot grate and place the ribs in your grill or smoker, meat side up. Cover and smoke for a total of 6 hours. After about 5 hours, begin to baste the ribs with the BBQ Sauce about every 20 minutes. The ribs are done when the meat cracks when picked up (with tongs) and they reach an internal temperature of 170 to 180°F.

4 To finish the ribs, throw them on the grill over direct medium heat to let the sauce caramelize. Baste between turns, and you're done.

TRIMMING YOUR RIBS: I SUPPOSE I'M THE BEST GUY to talk about ribs, though I should mention that I'm doing this under serious protest. St. Louis–style ribs are pork spareribs that have been trimmed of the rib tips and skirt to create a uniform rectangular shape. If you can't find St. Louis–style ribs in your market, ask your butcher to trim spareribs for you or prepare them yourself at home.

To prepare St. Louis–style ribs, place the spareribs bone-side up on a cutting board. Usually, there will be a flap of meat that runs along the slab, called the skirt. Remove the skirt; it can be cooked separately, and it's a very flavorful part of us pigs. Remove the excess fat.

Cut along the end of the rib bones, cutting between the bone and cartilage, to remove the irregular-shaped portion of meat attached to the ribs.

Remove the tough outer membrane. Slide a butter knife under the membrane and pry it up, then grab a hold of it with a clean paper towel and peel it off. Last, remove the rib tips (they can be cooked separately) and the opposite end to square up the rack.

BROTHER JIMMY'S

DRY (OR SOUTHERN) RUB RIBS

3 racks St. Louis–style ribs (see sidebar, page 115)

⅓ cup Brother Jimmy's Dry Rub (page 25) or Southern Rub (page 26)

SERVES 6 to 8

The method for making Brother Jimmy's Dry Rub Ribs and Southern Rub Ribs are the same; only the rub is different. The Dry Rub has a dozen different herbs and spices, and because it is made with fennel seed, it's reminiscent of Italian sausage. The Southern Rub is our Memphis-style rub, and it's a bit sweeter, though there's still some spice.

1 Pat the ribs dry, season with your choice of rub, and wrap the ribs in plastic. Refrigerate for at least 6 hours or up to overnight. About 30 minutes before you're ready to grill, pull the ribs out of the refrigerator and let them come to room temperature.

2 Prepare your smoker or grill for barbecuing, using the indirect heat setup (see page 15) with a drip pan in place, and preheat to 210°F.

3 Pour some water in the drip pan and place some presoaked wood chunks or a packet of presoaked wood chips directly on the hot coals. Oil the hot grate and place the ribs in your grill or smoker, meat side up. Cover and smoke for a total of 6 hours.

4 The ribs are done when the meat cracks when picked up (with tongs), and they reach an internal temperature of 170°F to 180°F.

PUERTO RICAN MOJO RIBS

When we began working on the menu for our first franchise location, in Puerto Rico, we thought it would be fun to give "local flavor" to our ribs, and this is what we came up with. The meat has a true island taste to it that can't be beat.

1 **Make the *mojo* rub:** In a small bowl, combine all ingredients for the rub.

2 **Make the *mojo* mop:** In a blender, combine all the ingredients for the mop except the onion and blend until the garlic and oregano are well chopped. Add the onion and refrigerate until ready to use.

3 Prepare your smoker or grill for barbecuing, using the indirect heat setup (see page 15) with a drip pan in place, and preheat to 210°F.

4 Pat the ribs dry then season with the *mojo* rub.

5 Pour some water in the drip pan and place some presoaked wood chunks or a packet of presoaked wood chips directly on the hot coals. Oil the hot grate and place the ribs in your grill or smoker, meat side up. Cover and smoke for a total of 6 hours. After about 5 hours, begin to baste the ribs with some of the *mojo* mop about every 20 minutes.

6 The ribs are done when the meat cracks when picked up (with tongs), and they reach an internal temperature of 170°F to 180°F.

7 Serve the ribs with the extra *mojo* mop.

FOR THE *MOJO* RUB:

1 tablespoon ground coriander

1½ teaspoons dark brown sugar

1 tablespoon kosher salt

1½ teaspoons ground black pepper

1½ teaspoons granulated onion

1½ teaspoons granulated garlic

1½ teaspoons dried oregano

FOR THE *MOJO* MOP:

4 garlic cloves

¼ cup packed fresh oregano leaves

1 cup fresh orange juice

¼ cup fresh lime juice

1 tablespoon kosher salt

1 teaspoon ground black pepper

1 teaspoon ground cumin

¼ cup olive oil

¼ cup minced red onion

3 racks St. Louis–style Ribs (see sidebar, page 115)

SERVES 6 to 8

BROTHER JIMMY'S
CAROLINA-STYLE
PULLED PORK

1 recipe Brother Jimmy's Dry Rub (page 25)

1 (6- to 8-pound) bone-in pork butt (also called pork shoulder or Boston butt)

1 cup Eastern Carolina BBQ Sauce (page 29), or to taste

SERVES 10 to 15

I'VE GOT TO clear up this misnomer. You're not actually eating the butt of a pig—'cause that'd be gross. This cut is from the upper portion of our shoulder. It has plenty of fat to stay moist during long, slow cooking, making it a favorite cut for barbecue. This cut comes bone-in, which is preferable to use for superior flavor and moisture retention, and boneless, which will range from about 5 to 8 pounds. If you can't find a bone-in pork butt, you may use boneless, though boneless meats cook faster than bone-in pieces.

This is a staple, and we go through most of it during our ultimate sporting events—UNC versus Duke basketball games, for example—but it can be enjoyed whenever, wherever. It's great on its own for example, or piled atop a bun with a little slaw for a delicious sandwich (as pictured here; see page 132 for the recipe). And, as a bonus, the blade bone can be used to flavor beans or soups.

1 Generously apply the rub to the pork, patting it on all over the surface of the meat.

2 Prepare your smoker or grill for barbecuing, using the indirect heat setup (see page 15) with a drip pan in place. Preheat to 220°F. Pour some water in the drip pan and place some presoaked wood chunks or a packet of presoaked wood chips directly on the hot coals. Just before you're ready to cook, oil the hot grate. Place the pork on the grate and cook, covered, for 6 to 8 hours, until the internal temperature is 175°F to 185°F. Some smokers cook hotter or more efficiently than others, so the exact cooking time will vary. After 6 hours, start checking the temperature. If it has reached 175°F to 185°F, the pork is done.

3 Remove the pork from the smoker and let it rest for about 15 minutes. Once the pork has rested, get ready to start pulling. First, remove the blade bone (simply tug it out). Pull apart the larger pieces of meat and put them into a large bowl. Try to remove as many of the large pieces of fat as you can and discard them.

4 Once all the meat is in the bowl, break it apart into smaller pieces. Add the Eastern Carolina BBQ Sauce and mix it all together to incorporate.

MUSTARD-RUBBED
WOOD-GRILLED
PORK
TENDERLOIN

If you have any leftovers, this grilled pork is great sliced up and tossed in a salad or between bread for a hearty sandwich.

1 Trim the silver skin and any excess fat off the pork and place in a gallon-size zip-top bag.

2 **Make the wet rub:** Place the garlic on a cutting board and smash it with the side of a large chef's knife. Place the salt on top of the smashed garlic and begin chopping together. Using the side of your knife, spread the garlic and salt around to smash it together. Continue smashing and chopping until you have a paste. (Salt acts like an abrasive, helping to grind the garlic to a smooth paste.) Place the garlic paste in a large bowl along with the remaining wet rub ingredients and mix well.

3 Add the wet rub to the pork, turning the pork until it is well coated. Get as much air out of the bag as you can, seal it up, and let it marinate in the refrigerator for 6 hours or up to overnight. About 45 minutes before you're ready to grill, pull the pork loin out of the refrigerator and let it come to room temperature.

4 Preheat your grill to moderate heat. Just before you're ready to cook, place presoaked wood chips or chunks (we recommend apple or cherry) on the hot coals and oil the grate.

5 Remove the pork from the bag, place it on the grill, and cook, covered, turning to mark all sides, for 10 to 15 minutes, until it registers an internal temperature of 140°F. Let it rest for 10 minutes before carving it.

2 pork tenderloins
(2 to 2½ pounds total)

FOR THE WET RUB:

3 garlic cloves

1 teaspoon kosher salt

⅓ cup grainy mustard

1 tablespoon Dijon mustard

2 tablespoons white wine

1½ teaspoons chopped fresh thyme

2 tablespoons olive oil

SERVES 6

PINEAPPLE RUM-GLAZED
PORK TENDERLOIN
WITH GRILLED PINEAPPLE

2 pork tenderloins
(2 to 2½ pounds total)

FOR THE PINEAPPLE-RUM MARINADE:

1 tablespoon brown sugar

¼ cup pineapple juice

¼ cup dark rum

2 tablespoons roughly chopped garlic

½ teaspoon salt

½ teaspoon ground black pepper

¼ cup olive oil

1 pineapple (golden variety if possible)

Salt and ground black pepper

Olive oil for drizzling

FOR THE PINEAPPLE-RUM GLAZE:

1 cup dark rum

½ cup pineapple juice

1 cup brown sugar

½ teaspoon salt

1 tablespoons fresh lime juice

Reserved marinade
(from above)

SERVES 6

Fruit and pork are a perfect marriage. Add rum and you have a flavorful threesome that can't be topped. Just make sure most of the rum makes it into the recipe.

1 Trim the silver skin and any excess fat off the pork and place it in a gallon-size zip-top bag.

2 **Make the marinade:** Combine the ingredients for the marinade in a small bowl and add to the bag with the pork. As you seal the bag, remove as much air as possible. Set in the refrigerator and marinate for up to 4 hours only. About 45 minutes before you're ready to grill, pull the pork loins out of the refrigerator and let them come to room temperature.

3 Peel and core the pineapple and slice into ¾- to 1-inch rings. Just before grilling, sprinkle a little salt, pepper, and oil.

4 **Make the glaze:** Combine the ingredients for the glaze in a small nonreactive saucepan and set aside.

5 Preheat your grill to moderate heat. Just before you're ready to cook, place presoaked wood chips or chunks (we recommend apple or cherry) on the hot coals and oil the grate.

6 Place the pork on the grill. Add the marinade to the saucepan with the glaze. Grill the pork, covered, turning to mark all sides with the grill. Simultaneously, start to grill the pineapple, marking it on both sides until it is hot, about 5 minutes.

7 When the pork registers 140°F internally, after 15 to 20 minutes, take it off the grill. Let it rest for 10 minutes before carving into it.

8 While the meat is resting, simmer the glaze and marinade mixture until it has thickened and reduced by about two-thirds.

9 Place the grilled pineapple on a platter with the sliced pork arranged beside it. Drizzle some of the glaze across the pork.

GRILLED
CHIPOTLE-ORANGE
PORK LOIN

This marinated and glazed pork loin goes well with our Pickled Red Onions (page 40). Because it's sweet and spicy, it'd also be great with our Warm Potato Salad (page 214), with a frosty beer beside the plate.

1 Remove any excess fat from the pork loin and set aside.

2 **Make the marinade:** Place the garlic on a cutting board and smash it with the side of a large chef's knife. Place the salt on top of the smashed garlic and begin chopping together. Using the side of your knife, spread the garlic and salt around to smash it together. Continue smashing and chopping until you have a paste. (Salt acts like an abrasive, helping to grind the garlic to a smooth paste.) Combine the garlic paste, Chipotle Puree, brown sugar, orange zest, orange juice, and oil in a bowl. Mix well, making sure to break up any lumps of brown sugar.

3 Place the pork loin in a gallon-size zip-top bag and pour in the marinade. Give it a shake and seal it tightly, squeezing out as much of the air as you can. Marinate 6 hours to overnight in the refrigerator. About 45 minutes before you're ready to grill, pull the pork loin out of the refrigerator and let it come to room temperature.

4 Preheat your grill to moderate heat. Just before you before you're ready to cook, oil the hot grates. Remove the pork from the bag (save the marinade), place on the grill, and close the grill cover. Turn the pork to mark on all sides and to avoid charring too much in one spot. Cook for 30 to 40 minutes, until an internal temperature of 140°F is reached. Remove from the grill and let it rest for 5 to 10 minutes before slicing.

5 **Make the chipotle-orange glaze:** Pour the saved marinade into a small saucepan and add the ½ cup orange juice. Bring to a boil, then reduce the heat and simmer for 10 minutes. Brush the chipotle-orange glaze all over the loin.

2 to 2½ pounds pork loin

FOR THE CHIPOTLE-ORANGE MARINADE:

2 garlic cloves

2 teaspoons salt

3 tablespoons Chipotle Puree (page 32)

2 tablespoons brown sugar

Zest of 2 oranges

¼ cup orange juice

3 tablespoons olive oil

FOR THE CHIPOTLE-ORANGE GLAZE:

Reserved marinade (from above)
½ cup orange juice

SERVES 6 to 8

BOURBON-MARINATED
PORK LOIN
WITH GRILLED PEACHES

1 (3-pound) boneless
pork loin roast

FOR THE MARINADE:

4 garlic cloves, chopped

¼ cup bourbon

2 teaspoons chopped
fresh thyme

2 teaspoons kosher salt

1½ teaspoons ground
black pepper

½ cup olive oil

2 tablespoons brown sugar

FOR THE PEACHES:

4 ripe peaches

1 teaspoon chopped
fresh thyme

Zest of ½ lemon

¼ cup olive oil

1 teaspoon kosher salt

1 teaspoon brown sugar

SERVES 6 to 8

In this dish, the bourbon shines through in the marinade and gives a nice little kick to the pork, balanced out by the sweetness of the ripe peaches. It's a perfect summer meal and tastes great cold atop a salad (we recommend using a peppery arugula).

1   Place the pork in a gallon-size zip-top bag or in a nonreactive container. Combine the ingredients for the marinade in a small bowl. Pour the marinade over the pork. (If using a bag, remove as much air as possible when sealing the bag.) Let it marinate for 4 hours in the refrigerator, turning or shaking it occasionally.

2   **Make the peaches:** About an hour before you're ready to grill the pork, set a pot of water to boil. Make a small X on the bottom of each peach with the tip of a sharp knife. Place the peaches carefully into the boiling water and let boil for a minute or two. (Don't let the peaches sit in the boiling water for too long—you don't want to cook them.) Remove and place in a bowl of ice water to cool quickly, then peel the skin off where you made the X. When the peaches are all peeled, cut them into quarters.

3   In a large bowl, combine the thyme, lemon zest, oil, salt, and brown sugar. Add the peach quarters and toss to evenly coat.

4   About 45 minutes before you're ready to grill, pull the pork out of the refrigerator and let come to room temperature.

5   Preheat your grill to moderate heat. Just before you're ready to cook, place presoaked wood chips or chunks on the hot coals and oil the hot grate. Cook the pork, covered, for about 45 minutes, until you have an internal temperature of 140°F. Let the pork rest while you prepare the peaches.

6   Remove the peaches from their marinade and mark each side on the grill until they are heated through.

7   Slice the pork and serve with the peaches.

TAILGATING GAMES: THIS MAY BE MY LEAST FAVORITE CHAPTER

in the book, but I'm still going to help you have a blast while you're tailgating by sharing some staple games folks can play. In fact, there are plenty of people who just go to tailgates in stadium lots with no intention of ever making it into the actual game. By no means should these showcases of drinking fortitude and shenanigans be limited merely to tailgating. Take it from someone who has a tail and knows best.

Some of the more popular games include: Cornhole, aka Bags (see page 146), Washer Pitching (picture Cornhole, but with oversize washers instead of bags), Flip Cup, Dizzy Bat, and Beer Pong.

FLIP CUP

is simple to set up, easy to play, yet hard to master. Line up two evenly numbered teams across a table and distribute a plastic cup to each player. Fill each with an equal amount of beer and then designate the starting side of the table and the ending side of the table. Once the game commences, participants have to chug their brew (avoid dousing the front of yourself because you're overeager—that's never a good look, and that's coming from a bona fide pig), then place the cup upside down on the edge of the table and flip it so it lands upright.

Once you've stuck the landing, the next person in line downs his or her beer and flips his or her cup. The winning team is the first one to make it through all their members. Repeat until your vision blurs. A little tip from ol' Reggie: Spill a drop or two of beer where you're about to flip—the liquid makes the cup adhere to the table better.

DIZZY BAT

is a fun little number in which the selected contestant gulps down a full beer out of the open end of a wiffle ball bat. Then that person has to spin around ten times with his forehead touching the end of the bat before attempting to hit a beer can pitched to him. If he swings and misses, he spins three more times before trying again.

Although the game is rather arduous for the participants, depending on how long the festivities have been going on for, it's utterly hilarious for the onlookers because most dizzy batters face-plant catastrophically, nearly wipe out onlookers, and generally meet the ground in an untimely, comical manner. Just remember that if you're going to lop off the end of the bat to drink from, you should smooth the edges down; no one wants to put his or her mouth where you've just bled.

BEER PONG

is addictively awesome, from what I've heard. I don't have thumbs, so I lack the dexterity to play. What makes the game so fun is the self-deluded idea that your skills rise as the rounds of games wear on. The setup is simple: six to ten cups filled with cheap beer (or fancy suds, if you're so inclined—and if so, please invite me over) in triangle formation on either side of a Ping-Pong table or any flat surface. Teams consist of at least two players on either side with two Ping-Pong balls between them.

The basic goal in every game is to eliminate all your opponents' cups before they do yours, without spilling. Every player should be aware of any "house rules," or personalized clauses added to the basic idea of the game, which may surprise a player at an inconvenient moment of the game, forcing him or her to lose a turn, or a cup. If you aren't sure, ask. There's nothing worse than being asked to re-rack your last cups into a diamond after losing two cups on a bounce-back because you left your beer unfinished, right? Because that'll happen if you don't ask. Trust me.

SMOKY CUBAN-STYLE PORK LOIN

1 (3- to 4-pound) boneless
pork loin roast

FOR THE MARINADE:

6 garlic cloves

1 tablespoon salt

½ cup finely chopped red onion

¼ cup fresh oregano leaves,
chopped

1 teaspoon ground black pepper

2 crumbled bay leaves

1 teaspoon ground cumin

1 teaspoon dried oregano

3 tablespoons fresh lime juice
(from about 1 large lime)

½ cup orange juice

2 tablespoons olive oil

SERVES 6 to 8

The flavor of this loin roast is similar to our Puerto Rican *Mojo* Ribs (page 117). It's great hot or cold, and is perfect for making Brother Jimmy's Cuban sandwich (page 130).

1 Place the pork in a gallon-size zip-top bag.

2 **Make the marinade:** Place the garlic on a cutting board and smash it with the side of a large chef's knife. Place the salt on top of the smashed garlic and begin chopping together. Using the side of your knife, spread the garlic and salt around to smash it together. Continue smashing and chopping until you have a paste. Add the garlic paste to the bag with the pork.

3 Place the remaining marinade ingredients in the bag and swish it around to mix well. Let marinate overnight in the refrigerator. About 45 minutes before you're ready to grill, pull the pork out of the refrigerator and let come to room temperature.

4 Prepare your smoker or grill for barbecuing, using the indirect heat setup (see page 15) with a drip pan in place, and preheat to 240°F. When you're ready to cook, pour some water into the drip pan, place some presoaked wood chunks or a packet of presoaked wood chips directly on the hot coals, and oil the hot grate. Cook the pork for about 2 hours, covered, until it reaches an internal temperature of 140°F to 150°F. Let the pork rest for about 10 minutes before cutting into it.

SOUTHERN SMOTHERED COUNTRY-STYLE RIBS

WITH ONION & BACON GRAVY

Served with a chunky gravy, seasoned with thyme and bay leaf, this home-style rustic dish is the perfect comfort food. And as it's rather simple and quick to make, you won't be laboring all day in the kitchen. If you don't have the time to make slow-cooked barbecue ribs, this rib recipe is a great alternative.

1 Slice the bacon into ½-inch pieces, place it in a large sauté pan, and place over low heat. Cook until it just starts to crisp around the edges.

2 Add the onion and thyme sprigs. Continue cooking over low heat until the onion becomes very soft and caramelizes.

3 Sprinkle the flour over the caramelized onion and cook, stirring well, to make a roux.

4 Warm the chicken stock and slowly add it a little at a time, mixing well after each addition. Once all the stock is added, simmer for about 10 minutes, add the salt and pepper, and remove from the heat.

5 Season the ribs with a little salt and pepper. Heat the oil in a large sauté pan over medium-high heat. Place the ribs in the pan, lower the heat to medium, and cook on all sides for about 9 minutes, until they are done, when their internal temperature reaches 140°F.

6 Place the ribs on a platter and smother them with the gravy.

6 slices bacon (regular or applewood smoked)

1 extra-large Spanish onion, thinly sliced

2 or 3 sprigs fresh thyme

3 tablespoons all-purpose flour

1 bay leaf

2 cups chicken stock (store-bought is fine)

½ teaspoon kosher salt, plus more for seasoning the ribs

½ teaspoon ground black pepper, plus more for seasoning the ribs

3 pounds boneless country-style pork ribs

3 tablespoons olive oil

SERVES 6

PORK CHOPS

STUFFED
WITH COUNTRY SAUSAGE & ANCHO CHILES

6 (1-inch-thick) center-cut pork chops (bone-in or boneless)

FOR THE STUFFING:

1 tablespoon olive oil

½ cup minced Spanish onion

3 garlic cloves, minced

½ teaspoon ancho chile powder

1 tablespoon chopped fresh thyme

½ teaspoon salt

6 ounces breakfast sausage, patties or links

2 tablespoons olive oil

Salt and ground black pepper

SERVES 6

Double the pork, double your pleasure! This recipe is great and easy to do on the grill, but it's just as good in a pan. The heat from the chiles isn't so overpowering that you'll miss the delicate flavor of the pork chop.

1 Take a pork chop and place it on a cutting board. With a very sharp boning knife or paring knife held parallel to the chop, make a small slit and move the knife around inside the chop, making a pocket—just be careful not to poke through the other side. Repeat with the remaining chops.

2 **Make the stuffing:** Heat a sauté pan over medium heat and add the 1 tablespoon oil. Add the onion, garlic, and ancho chile powder and sauté until the onion is translucent, about 5 minutes. Remove from the heat and add the thyme and salt. Transfer to a bowl to cool.

3 Break up the sausage into the stuffing mixture and mix well.

4 Preheat your grill to moderate heat and have some presoaked wood chunks or a packet of wood chips ready to hit the flames.

5 While the grill is heating up, divide the sausage stuffing into 6 equal parts. Taking a little at a time, stuff each chop. When they are all stuffed, take a toothpick and stick it through the meat, diagonally across the slit. With another toothpick, do the same in the opposite direction to create a wide X, sealing the hole.

6 When all the chops are stuffed and sealed, rub the 2 tablespoons of oil over them and sprinkle with salt and pepper.

7 Just before you before you're ready to cook, oil the hot grates. Grill for 6 to 7 minutes per side, to an internal temperature of 150°F, taking care to cook through the raw sausage in the center.

BREAKOUT RECIPES

GREAT SANDWICHES

You're bound to have a mound of leftover pork if you're making these recipes, and one of the best uses for excess swine is to pile it between some bread for sandwiches. While the possibilities of fillings are literally limitless, depending on how crafty and creative you are, we've got three great sandwich recommendations for you. More over, peanut butter and jelly; you just got one-upped.

BROTHER JIMMY'S CUBAN

4 tablespoons (½ stick) unsalted butter, softened

2 ½ tablespoons Dijon mustard

¼ teaspoon finely minced garlic

Pinch of salt

1 loaf French bread (at least 20 inches)

½ pound Swiss cheese, sliced

⅓ pound thinly sliced ham

24 pickle chips or Frickles (page 76)

½ pound smoked pork butt (see Note) or Cuban-Style Pork Loin (page 126), thinly sliced

Vegetable or olive oil for brushing the top and bottom of sandwich

1 Combine the butter, mustard, garlic, and salt in a small bowl and stir until well combined.

2 Slice the loaf lengthwise all the way through and spread the mustard-garlic butter on both sides. Lay the cheese along the length of the bread, followed by the ham, pickle chips, then the pork.

3 Cut the loaf into four equal pieces, then brush with oil. Cook in a panini press following the manufacturer's instructions, or cook on low to medium heat on a preheated griddle or large frying pan, with a weighted-down pan on top. When the cheese starts to melt, the Cuban is ready to eat.

SERVES 4 to 8

NOTE If you're using smoked pork butt for this sandwich, simply follow the recipe for Brother Jimmy's Carolina-Style Pulled Pork (page 118), but don't pull or sauce the pork.

BROTHER JIMMY'S CUBAN

BLFGT
(BACON, LETTUCE, FRIED GREEN TOMATO)

BLFGT (BACON, LETTUCE, FRIED GREEN TOMATO)

FOR THE FRIED GREEN TOMATO COATING:

1 cup cornmeal

1 cup plain breadcrumbs

1½ teaspoons salt

1 tablespoon ground black pepper

1 tablespoon celery salt

1 cup all-purpose flour

2 large eggs

1 cup buttermilk

18 slices applewood-smoked bacon
(or any other smoky bacon)

1 to 2 cups canola oil for frying

4 green tomatoes, sliced about ¼ inch thick

Hellman's mayonnaise

12 slices country white bread

6 large lettuce leaves (we prefer romaine)

. . . .

1 Preheat the oven to 350°F.

2 Put all the ingredients for the fried green tomato coating in a bowl and mix well to combine. Put the flour in a shallow bowl. In a separate shallow bowl, beat the eggs with the buttermilk.

3 Lay the bacon on a baking sheet (with sides) and bake in for 10 to 13 minutes, until crisp. Blot on paper towels to remove extra grease and let cool.

4 While the bacon is cooking, begin to make the fried green tomatoes. Pour 1 cup of the oil into a large sauté pan (preferably cast iron) and set over medium heat. You will need 2 to 3 slices of green tomato per sandwich depending on the size of the tomatoes.

5 Begin by dredging the tomato slices first in the flour, then the egg mixture, and then in the coating mixture, coating the slices well. Fry the tomatoes in several batches (take care to set them gently in the oil, away from you, to avoid splatters) so as not to overcrowd the pan, about 1½ minutes per side, until they are golden and crisp. Add more oil to the pan as needed and drain the fried tomatoes on paper towels.

6 To assemble the sandwiches, spread the mayonnaise on both sides of the bread, top each with 2 or 3 fried tomato slices, 3 slices of bacon, and a leaf of lettuce.

SERVES 6

THE CLASSIC PULLED PORK WITH SLAW

Brother Jimmy's Carolina-Style Pulled Pork (page 118)

Creamy Slaw (page 47)

10 soft sandwich rolls

Eastern Carolina BBQ Sauce (page 29), for serving

Pickles, for serving

. . . .

1 Place a nice mound of pulled pork in each roll and top it with some slaw. Keep some extra BBQ sauce on hand for extra saucing.

2 Serve it up with a plate of pickles.

SERVES 10 or more

DRINKS: THESE CONCOCTIONS will work perfectly for your tailgating party:

MINT JULEP

(Hair of the Dog) —This is our version of the mint julep. These go down quick and easy during any event, but are especially nice and refreshing during a hot afternoon of tailgating. See the recipe on page 67.

CHARLESTON A.P.

Remember the Arnold Palmer? Let's spike that bad boy. Half lemonade, half sweet-tea-flavored vodka, and you have the Charleston A.P. Because vodka can make any beverage better. See the recipe on page 54.

RISE & SHINE

This concoction is made with orange juice, so you get your vitamin C, and it's perfect for the "gating" because you can drink it pretty early on in the day. It's a good start-off beverage before you get into the full swing of things. See the recipe on page 66.

TAILGATING CHECKLIST: UNSURE OF WHAT TO PACK for your tailgate? Here's my handy little checklist of the bare necessities:

☐ **A SMALL GRILL.** You can pick them up for under 30 bucks at places like Walmart, Kmart, or any other mart.

☐ **FUEL FOR THE GRILL.** Whatever the source of heat may be, make sure you can keep the fire sufficiently fed while you're out in the parking lot. No one ever wants to make a run to the store for more propane halfway into a good tailgate.

☐ **WOOD CHIPS OR CHUNKS FOR SMOKING.** If you're doing something that involves smoldering wood, you'd best have wood on hand that's able to smolder beneath your meat. Any wood will do, just make sure you've got enough so you don't run out.

☐ **ENOUGH FOOD** for wanderers. People are going to stop by and hang out. Make sure you have enough eats and drinks to share with your newfound friends. And when you finally run out of supplies, then it's obviously your turn to stroll the lot looking for some freebies.

☐ **SALT.** In addition to helping season the grub, it can double as a quick way to get beers in your cooler ice cold. See page 148 for that fun tip.

☐ **PLATES, CUPS, AND UTENSILS.** Gotta have the various vessels for carrying the fare and libations, right? Don't forget napkins, unless you want to wipe barbecue sauce directly on your jersey.

☐ **TEAM PARAPHERNALIA.** Half the fun of the tailgate is drinking and eating; the other half is seeing how insane fellow fans can get with the team spirit. Feel free to adorn your car/body/face with your team's flags, logos, and colors. And if you're going to face paint, please do it while you're still sober. Your penmanship deteriorates quickly as the day wears on. No need to walk around with half a mascot smeared on your forehead.

☐ **ACCOUTREMENTS FOR DRINKING GAMES.** Be it a pigskin (does everything have to be named after my kind?), a Frisbee, a table for Flip Cup, or a bat for Dizzy Bat, make sure you have the right supplies to occupy yourself and your crew.

BEEF

THE SCENE IS A FAMILIAR ONE:

A BACKYARD BARBECUE BASH, WITH GUESTS

milling around the pool, soaking up spring and summer rays, sunglasses on, frosty beers or cocktails in hand. Music blasts, games of horseshoes or bocce are in full swing, and the mood is upbeat and lively. Tantalizing scents of cooking beef waft over when the wind blows in the right direction as a steady plume of smoke rises from the grill, signifying a scrumptious meal isn't long off.

There's something inherently rustic about the backyard barbecue. From the simplicity of the cooking process—just the core essentials of heat and smoke are necessary—to the no-frills paper plates waiting to take on the challenge of staying rigid under the mountain of piping hot food they're about to carry precariously. It's all stripped down because good barbecue doesn't need a ton of additives and ingredients to be tasty. It's a mind-set we practice daily in our kitchens when dealing with our beef.

Your beef—whatever cut or type it may be—is always hoisted to the table in a triumphant fashion, as if to say, "Look at this meat. Look what we've created. We rule," before the ceremonial slicing begins. Expectant mouths water with anticipation, and it seems like mere seconds until the platter is cleaned off. The meat is so tender, metal silverware is wholly unnecessary. The only sound audible is now the music, as revelers' mouths are far too full for conversation. Unless, of course, it's to inquire if seconds are an immediate option.

The ethos of the backyard barbecue is one we replicate each night in our Brother Jimmy's restaurants. The vibrancy and energy that comes from a grill-side gathering of your friends and family is what we're best at capturing. We see it daily during our happy hours, when smiles and laughter abound and the drinks are flowing. People don't need frills and extras to have a good time. Beyond great food, the only requisites are some alcohol, great tracks booming from speakers, and a few friends. And just like in your backyard, in our restaurants we don't mind a lull in chatter, if it means you're too busy savoring what's on your plate.

Because we're a North Carolina restaurant at heart, we tend to focus on pork (those recipes are in the previous chapter). That's because pork fills the bulk of smokers in North Carolina, a region that historically has had more pigs than any other in the United States. But we'd never

overlook the grill's other favorite companion: beef. It makes sense that in Texas, a leading producer of the nation's cattle, beef reigns supreme. Not surprisingly, it's the standard item routinely gracing the bulk of the menu in any barbecue joint in the state.

So it's safe to say we appreciate a perfectly smoked brisket, either lean or marbled, and our customers do, too—we sell approximately 1,900 pounds per week in our restaurants. We plate up countless smoked beef short ribs and slice our BBQ meatloaf (wrapped in bacon, naturally) with alarming speed. We've got beef down pat, and we're about to open our storied beef recipes to you.

In its essence, beef is a versatile product that easily translates to home entertaining. Grind it up and pack it into a baking pan for loaves or mold it into patties for burgers. Slice off a steak. Cut the bone away from a rib steak. Then smoke it, grill it, sauté it, fry it, bake it, braise it, roast it, or stew it—whatever your little heart desires. It'll all end up in the same place: your belly.

WHICH MAKES BEEF THE PERFECT BACKYARD BARBEQUE FOOD. YOU CAN ALWAYS FIND SOME FORM OF it to satiate your guests, and it's the kind of smoking and grilling that doesn't necessarily require constant attention and care.

Which makes beef the perfect backyard barbecue food. You can always find some form of it to satiate your guests, and it's the kind of smoking and grilling that doesn't necessarily require constant attention and care. A few checks here and there to make sure you're not completely charring everything and you can be off partying with your friends and family for most of the day. Nothing's easier than our Southern Skirt Steak with Blackened Onions, which literally calls for only salt, pepper, and oil. The beauty of this cut is that it tastes good even if you happen to overcook it. It's truly foolproof meat. Everyone'll know when it's mealtime when they hear the reassuring sizzle of freshly turned steak undergoing a final check from the grill master.

At the restaurant, we've got a few beef dishes that don't require briquettes and a searing grill to make, and those are included here as well. Like our Country-Fried Steak with White Gravy, a true Southern institution. We get the cube steak so tenderized before its bath in flour and egg and hot oil that the meat often falls apart when it meets your fork.

So fish another cold beer out of the ice chest, mix up a pitcher of libations, grab a choice cut of beef, and fire up the grill (or your stove or oven). Fair warning: It won't take long before your neighbors start to drift over, drawn by the alluring smells, so have some extra plates handy. Though if you're not a big fan of invading passersby, better invest in a sturdy fence to keep the hungry masses at bay.

PLAYLIST

A nice mixture of upbeat country and classic rock will be sure to keep your backyard barbecue energized. This backyard, happy-hour musical category is right in Brother Jimmy's wheelhouse. Beer, the outdoors, the sizzling grill, and summertime are all perfectly captured in these tracks.

THE ALLMAN BROTHERS
BLUE SKY

BIG HEAD TODD AND THE MONSTERS
BROKEN HEARTED SAVIOR

BRUCE SPRINGSTEEN
THUNDER ROAD

STEVIE RAY VAUGHAN
COULDN'T STAND THE WEATHER

DRIVE-BY TRUCKERS
MY SWEET ANNETTE

GARTH BROOKS
AIN'T GOING DOWN

JIMMY BUFFETT
VOLCANO

TOBY KEITH
BEER FOR MY HORSES

KID ROCK
ALL SUMMER LONG

KENNY CHESNEY
BEER IN MEXICO

LYNYRD SKYNYRD
GIMME THREE STEPS

JOHN FOGARTY
CENTERFIELD

THE ROLLING STONES
MONKEY MAN

DIRE STRAITS
WALK OF LIFE

RED HOT CHILI PEPPERS
DANI CALIFORNIA

THE BEATLES
DAY TRIPPER

ALAN JACKSON
WHERE I COME FROM

JOHNNY CASH
RING OF FIRE

THE CHARLIE DANIELS BAND
LONG HAIRED COUNTRY BOY

SHERYL CROW
SOAK UP THE SUN

THE BLACK CROWES
TWICE AS HARD

TOM PETTY
MARY JANE'S LAST DANCE

DIERKS BENTLEY
HOW AM I DOIN'?

PHIL VASSAR
SIX-PACK SUMMER

TRAVIS TRITT
MODERN DAY BONNIE & CLYDE

SMOKED

BRISKET

Brisket is the hallmark of Texas 'cue. Made up of layers of fat and muscle, it can be one of the toughest cuts of beef around, if not prepared properly. If given plenty of cooking time to break down its dense connective tissue, it's one of the most flavorful and tender beef experiences you'll ever have—well worth the wait. In our restaurants we sprinkle it with Brisket Sugar Shake to round out the flavor. You can also smoke it "naked," as they do in Texas, or try it with our Original BBQ Sauce (page 31).

1 (4- to 6-pound) brisket, untrimmed, with a thick sheath of fat

5 tablespoons brown sugar

5 tablespoons kosher salt

1 tablespoon ground black pepper

4½ teaspoons paprika

1½ teaspoons dry mustard

1 tablespoon ancho chile powder

½ teaspoon granulated onion

¼ teaspoon granulated garlic

Brisket Sugar Shake (page 28) for serving

SERVES 6 to 8

1 Trim the brisket, leaving ¼ inch of fat. Lightly score the fat so the rub can sink in.

2 In a medium bowl, combine the remaining ingredients (except the sugar shake) and thoroughly rub over the brisket. Wrap the meat in plastic and refrigerate for at least 6 hours or up to overnight. About 45 minutes before you're ready to grill, pull the brisket out of the refrigerator and let come to room temperature.

3 Prepare your smoker or grill for barbecuing, using the indirect heat setup (see page 15) with a drip pan in place, and preheat to 190°F. Pour some water in the drip pan and place some presoaked wood chunks or a packet of presoaked wood chips directly on the hot coals. Oil the hot grate and place the brisket in fat side up and smoke, covered, for 1 to 1¼ hours per pound. This could take as little as 5 hours or as many as 10. You want the brisket to reach an internal temperature of 180°F to 185°F.

4 Let the brisket rest for a few minutes before cutting into it. Remember to always cut across the grain. Finish with a sprinkle of the Brisket Sugar Shake.

BRISKET:

Brisket comes in two basic cuts: the flat cut, which has minimal fat; and the point cut, sometimes called packer-trimmed, which has more fat. You want the fattier cut, which may mean placing a special order with your butcher to get it.

SMOKED
BEEF SHORT RIBS
WITH BOURBON BBQ SAUCE

5 tablespoons brown sugar

5 tablespoons kosher salt

1 tablespoon ground
black pepper

4½ teaspoons paprika

1½ teaspoons dry mustard

1 tablespoon ancho
chile powder

½ teaspoon granulated onion

¼ teaspoon granulated garlic

4 pounds beef short ribs,
3 to 4 inches long

1 to 2 cups Bourbon BBQ Sauce
(page 30)

SERVES 6

It's not every day that you eat a cut of meat as well marbled as this, so we say screw your cholesterol count and fast all day to make room.

1 In a medium bowl, combine all the ingredients except the ribs and the sauce. Rub the short ribs with the spice mixture. Cover and refrigerate overnight. About 30 minutes before you're ready to grill, pull the short ribs out of the refrigerator and let come to room temperature.

2 Prepare your smoker or grill for barbecuing, using the indirect heat setup (see page 15) with a drip pan in place, and preheat to between 190°F and 200°F. Just before cooking, pour some water in the drip pan, place some presoaked wood chunks or a packet of presoaked wood chips directly on the hot coals, and oil the hot grate. Smoke the short ribs, covered, for 5 to 6 hours, until the meat becomes tender and reaches an internal temperature of about 170°F to 180°F, basting with the Bourbon BBQ Sauce during the last hour or so.

3 To finish, we like to throw the ribs on the grill over direct medium heat, basting with more sauce to caramelize.

BBQ MEATLOAF

½ cup diced applewood-smoked bacon (or any other smoky bacon) plus 12 whole slices

½ cup diced Spanish onion

4 garlic cloves, chopped

1 cup panko (Japanese breadcrumbs)

¼ cup milk

2 large eggs

½ cup ketchup

½ cup Brother Jimmy's Original BBQ Sauce (page 31), plus extra for basting

1 tablespoon Dijon mustard

1 tablespoon Worcestershire sauce

1 teaspoon chopped fresh parsley

1 teaspoon chopped fresh thyme

1 teaspoon ground black pepper

1¾ pounds ground beef

¾ pound ground pork

SERVES 6 to 8

There is little more comforting than meatloaf, and we have upped the ante by wrapping it in bacon and smoking it low and slow on the grill.

1 Preheat your grill to moderate heat.

2 Place the diced bacon in a sauté pan and set over medium heat. Cook until the fat begins to render, about 5 minutes, then add the onion and garlic and cook until the onion softens, about 5 minutes. Remove from the heat and cool.

3 In a small bowl, combine the panko and milk. Set aside.

4 In a large bowl, combine the eggs, ketchup, BBQ sauce, mustard, Worcestershire sauce, parsley, thyme, and pepper. Add the soaked panko, then add the bacon mixture and the ground beef and pork.

5 Lay out the bacon slices on a baking rack, just slightly overlapping. Shape the meat mixture on the center of the bacon; it should be about 12 inches long. Fold the bacon around the meatloaf, then carefully roll the loaf so that the bacon "seam" is on the bottom. Place the baking rack onto another pan to catch the drippings and prevent flare-ups.

6 Just before cooking, pour some water in the drip pan, place some presoaked wood chunks (applewood or maple work great) or a packet of presoaked wood chips directly on the hot coals, and oil the hot grate.

7 Place the pan with the baking rack and meatloaf on the grill and cook, covered, for about 15 minutes, then begin basting the meatloaf with BBQ Sauce. Use a silicone brush or a traditional mop for best results. Continue cooking and basting until the internal temperature reaches 160°F. (This can take 45 to 90 minutes, but will depend on your equipment. Go by internal temperature, not time.)

8 Remove from the grill and let rest for about 5 minutes.

SOUTHERN
SKIRT STEAK
WITH BLACKENED ONIONS

We like to do this all on the grill, but you can also blacken the onions in a grill pan on the stovetop just as easily. When prepared simply, skirt steak is one of the most flavorful, yet cheapest, cuts of beef.

3 pounds skirt steak

¼ cup olive oil, plus more for coating the steak

½ teaspoon salt, plus more for seasoning the steak

Ground black pepper

2 large Spanish onions

3 to 4 tablespoons Blackening Spice (page 29)

½ teaspoon salt

SERVES 6 to 8

1 Preheat your grill to high heat.

2 Trim any excessive fat and sinew off the steak. Lightly coat with oil and season liberally with salt and pepper.

3 Slice the onions into ½-inch rounds and lay them on a tray in one layer. Do your best to keep the rings intact—they will fall apart eventually, but it's easier to get a nice char when the rounds are in one piece. Drizzle the onions with the ¼ cup oil, then sprinkle the Blackening Spice evenly over them.

4 Just before you before you're ready to cook, oil the hot grates. Place the onions on the grill and—if your grill is big enough—get the steak on as well.

5 When the onions look like they are starting to char on one side, about 4 to 5 minutes, carefully flip them over.

6 The steak cooks approximately 5 minutes per side for medium rare, depending on thickness.

7 As the onions char on each side, remove them to a bowl. When all the onions are off the grill, sprinkle with the salt.

8 After removing the steak, let it rest for 10 minutes before cutting into it. Cut it on an angle, across the grain.

9 Lay the steak on a platter with the blackened onions alongside.

COUNTRY-FRIED STEAK
WITH WHITE GRAVY

A true Southern staple, this dish can be served at any meal—even for breakfast alongside some eggs. A quick tip: After pounding out the beef, when you're certain it's thin enough, give it five more solid whacks. This is a tough piece of meat, and you want it tender. And don't worry if holes form in the meat; they give it character.

1 Combine the flour, salt, pepper, and granulated garlic in a shallow pan.

2 Lay the cube steaks out and pound them with a meat pounder or mallet until the meat is about 1/8 inch thick.

3 In a separate shallow pan, lightly beat the eggs, buttermilk, and Tabasco sauce.

4 Take the pounded steaks and dredge them in the seasoned flour, shake them, then dip them into the egg wash. Return them to the flour for a second dredging, making sure they are well coated.

5 Heat 1 cup of the oil in a heavy-bottomed pan (cast iron is ideal) over medium heat. Working in batches, carefully place the steaks in the oil and fry for about 3 minutes per side. Add more oil as needed. Serve with the white gravy.

3 cups all-purpose flour

2 tablespoons salt

4½ teaspoons ground black pepper

2¼ teaspoons granulated garlic

2 to 3 pounds cube steak

3 large eggs

2 cups buttermilk

2 drops Tabasco sauce

1 to 2 cups canola oil for frying

White Gravy for serving (recipe follows)

SERVES 6

4 cups milk

½ teaspoon chicken base

½ teaspoon ground dried sage

¼ teaspoon dried thyme

Pinch of white pepper

½ teaspoon ground
black pepper

1½ teaspoons salt

3 tablespoons unsalted butter

7 tablespoons all-purpose flour

MAKES 4 ½ cups

WHITE GRAVY

1 In a 2-quart saucepan, combine the milk, chicken base, sage, thyme, white pepper, black pepper, and salt. Place over medium-high heat and bring just to a boil.

2 In a separate saucepan, melt the butter over low heat and whisk in the flour. Cook, stirring, for 1 minute to make a roux.

3 Slowly pour the hot milk mixture into the roux, increase the heat slightly, and continue mixing until the gravy thickens considerably.

4 Serve over Country-Fried Steak (page 145) or mashed potatoes.

BACKYARD GAMES: THE BACKYARD IS THE PERFECT BACKDROP

for friendly competition among friends. And by friendly, I mean rivalry so fierce you'd rather draw blood than lose. Try these classic outdoor games at your next bash.

BADMINTON:

Show off your racquet skills by swatting the birdie over the net. You can play doubles or singles, and the match goes to whoever first reaches 21 points per game (best of three games). The rules and game play are just like tennis, except you get to shout out phrases like "Give me back the shuttlecock!"

VOLLEYBALL:

I'm really into volleyball because I like all the sand most courts have; it reminds me of my pen. You can use the same net, for badminton, just raise it up a bit. Grab six friends and start bumping, setting, and spiking. The team who wins the best of three games to 15 points takes the trophy (read: case of beer).

BOCCE: This game, thought to

be from the Roman Empire, is pretty simple. I call it "lawn bowling" around the sty. You'll need a set of Bocce balls (which is ironic, because *bocce* means "balls" in Italian), and a sizeable playing space. Toss the jack, or the small ball, down to one end, then teams take turns bowling four bigger balls toward it. Points are awarded to whoever is nearest the jack at the end of the round.

HORSESHOES:

Should you find yourself de-shoeing a horse, hang on to the irons and start a horseshoe pit in your yard. Drive a few spikes into the ground about 50 feet apart, take aim, and toss your shoes, trying for the holy grail of the sport: a dead ringer (when your shoe completely wraps around the pole).

CORNHOLE (OR BAGS): Go ahead, giggle at the

name. But this is a game that can be traced back to fifteenth-century England and has a history tangled in folklore and mystery. The game is broken down into innings, during which there is a top and bottom round, like baseball, except heckling may have a greater effect here. Two raised planks of wood with a hole cut out sitting precisely twenty-seven feet apart make up the playing field. Each player or team uses four corn bags, or bean bags, which they toss at the hole. Points are awarded based on where the bag lands in proximity to the hole. The first competitor to reach 21 without going over wins. You can also wing the bags at your opponents while they're tossing to make it that much more competitive/painful.

BOURBON MOLASSES POT ROAST

Pot roast is a great way to take a tough piece of beef and make it extremely tender. The bourbon kicks up the sauce a notch or seven, so don't be afraid to add a smidgen more to the pot. And, of course, pour yourself a glass while you're cooking.

1 Season the roast with salt and pepper. Heat the oil in a Dutch oven (or any heavy-duty pot with a secure lid) over medium-high heat and brown the roast on all sides.

2 Remove the meat to a plate and place the onion, garlic, and carrot in the pot. Reduce the heat to medium and sauté for about 10 minutes, stirring, until the vegetables begin to soften.

3 Add 1 cup of the bourbon, the stock, molasses, Worcestershire sauce, and bay leaf and bring to a boil. Cook for 5 minutes, then return the roast to the pot, return the mixture to a boil, and cover.

4 Lower the heat as low as it will go and cook for about 3 hours, until tender—the time will vary depending on the size or your roast.

5 When the meat is fork tender, remove it from the pot and let it rest on a cutting board for about 5 to 10 minutes.

6 While the meat is resting, add the remaining 2 tablespoons bourbon and the ¼ teaspoon of salt to the pot, increase the heat to high, and cook for 5 minutes to reduce the sauce a bit.

7 Slice the pot roast and serve with the cooking liquid.

1 (3- to 5-pound) chuck roast, tied

¼ teaspoon salt, plus more for seasoning the roast

Ground black pepper

2 tablespoons olive oil

2 cups minced Spanish onion

4 garlic cloves, chopped

1 cup minced carrot

1 cup plus 2 tablespoons bourbon

2 cups chicken or beef stock (store-bought is fine)

½ cup molasses

1 tablespoon Worcestershire sauce

1 bay leaf

SERVES 6 to 8

GRILLED RIB EYE

WITH CHIPOTLE BUTTER

FOR THE CHIPOTLE BUTTER:

¾ cup (1½ sticks) unsalted butter, at room temperature

3 tablespoons Chipotle Puree (page 32)

½ teaspoon salt

FOR THE STEAKS:

2 tablespoons smoked paprika

1 tablespoon chili powder

1 tablespoon granulated onion

1 teaspoon ground cumin

1 teaspoon ground coriander

2 tablespoons salt

6 (1-inch-thick) bone-in or boneless rib-eye steaks

SERVES 6

When you take a heavily marbled cut of meat with a really rich, beefy flavor and top it with chipotle butter, which adds a nice bit of sweet heat, the result is heaven in your mouth.

1 **Make the chipotle butter:** In a small bowl, blend the butter with the chipotle puree and salt and set aside.

2 **Make the steaks:** In a small bowl, combine the paprika, chili powder, granulated onion, cumin, coriander, and salt. Rub into the steaks, cover, and refrigerate for about 2 hours. About 30 minutes before you're ready to grill, pull the steaks out of the refrigerator and let come to room temperature.

3 Preheat your grill to medium-high. Just before before you're ready to cook, oil the hot grates. Grill the steaks for 4 to 5 minutes per side for medium rare or longer if you prefer well done. Serve with a spoonful of chipotle butter on top.

ICE COLD BEER: GOOD OLE REGGIE'S got a great trick for you for cooling beer. I'm partial to Natty Light or Pabst Blue Ribbon, because they're cheap when bought in cases, always go down easy, and you can build a fort out of all the empty cans afterward. Regardless of the suds filling your mugs, opt for cans over bottles, and here's why: You can get a can of brew ice cold in less than four minutes, if you know a little secret.

Grab your warm cans and dump them into a metal pot or bucket. Fill the container to the top with ice, then water. Now add about 2 cups of table salt (the secret ingredient), stir until the salt dissolves, and toss in the freezer—if you can. Wait about four minutes and your previously warm cans of beer will be so cold they'll stick to your snout. This method also doubles as a fun wager with your guests. Bet someone you can get a beer cold faster than they can. Loser buys the next case, naturally.

BBQ FAJITAS

2 pounds flank steak, trimmed of excess fat and sinew

FOR THE MARINADE:

2 tablespoons chopped garlic

¼ cup brown sugar

1½ cups amber ale

3 tablespoons molasses

2 tablespoons lime juice

4 teaspoons salt

1 teaspoon ground black pepper

4 teaspoons ancho chile powder

½ teaspoon cayenne pepper

1 teaspoon ground coriander

FOR THE GRILLED VEGGIES:

3 bell peppers (mix and match colors—use at least 1 red for some sweetness), stemmed, seeded, and quartered

2 red onions, sliced into ¼-inch rounds

3 jalapeños

½ cup olive oil

¼ cup Brother Jimmy's Southern Rub (page 26)

FOR BARBECUE SOUR CREAM:

8 ounces sour cream

¼ cup Brother Jimmy's Original BBQ Sauce (page 31)

¼ teaspoon salt

★

½ cup olive oil

18 (6-inch) flour tortillas

SERVES 6

Fajitas are fun to do with a lot of people hanging around the grill. The meat's coming off and lots of helping hands are around, throwing everything together before it hits the plate.

1 Place the steak in a large zip-top bag or nonreactive container. Combine the ingredients for the marinade in a bowl. Pour over the steak and marinate for at least 3 hours, up to overnight, in the refrigerator.

2 About 30 minutes before you're ready to grill, pull the steak out of the refrigerator and let come to room temperature. Preheat your grill to medium-high and soak some wood chips.

3 Meanwhile, toss together all of the ingredients for the grilled veggies in a large bowl and set aside. In another bowl, combine the ingredients for the sour cream.

4 Place the wood chips in a foil packet, pierce a few holes on top, and place on the fire. Take the meat out of its marinade and toss it with the ½ cup of oil. Oil the hot grate and grill the meat for 5 to 7 minutes on each side. Place the sliced onion on the grill. Once you have turned the steak, put the peppers on the grill; cook for a couple of minutes on each side, until they have nice grill marks.

5 Remove the meat and let rest for about 5 minutes, then thinly slice against the grain. Cut the onion rounds in half and the peppers into ¼-inch strips. Cut the core and seeds out of the jalapeños and cut into very thin strips; toss together.

6 Warm the tortillas on the grill. To assemble, spread some of the sour cream on a tortilla, lay a couple slices of steak on top, followed by some of the peppers and onion. Repeat with the remaining tortillas.

WET-RUBBED SIRLOIN

WITH HOMEMADE STEAK SAUCE

The wet rub really sets this sirloin apart, with all the herbs and garlic melding together flawlessly. The homemade steak sauce is quick and easy to make and can come in handy for nearly anything else you'll whip up in the kitchen. Like on your fries, burgers, or mashed potatoes. Except for cereal; we don't recommend putting it on your Wheaties.

1 recipe Fresh Herb and Garlic Rub (page 28)

1 (3- to 4-pound) sirloin steak

FOR THE STEAK SAUCE:

1 slice applewood-smoked bacon, cut into 6 pieces

¼ cup diced onion

3 garlic cloves, smashed

¾ cup water

3 tablespoons Worcestershire sauce

2 tablespoons cider vinegar

4½ teaspoons soy sauce

½ teaspoon dry mustard

¼ teaspoon granulated onion

⅛ teaspoon ground cinnamon

2 small white mushrooms

½ cup ketchup

4½ teaspoons brown sugar

SERVES 6 to 8

1 Rub the Fresh Herb and Garlic Rub into the steak, cover, and refrigerate for 2 to 4 hours. About 30 minutes before you're ready to grill, pull the steak out of the refrigerator and let come to room temperature.

2 Preheat your grill to medium heat. Have presoaked wood chips or chunks ready to throw onto the hot coals.

3 **Make the steak sauce:** Brown the bacon in a 1-quart saucepan over low heat. Add the onion and garlic. Add the remaining steak sauce ingredients, bring to a simmer, and cook for 10 to 15 minutes, until the sauce thickens slightly.

4 Pour the contents of the pan into a blender and blend until smooth, holding the lid tightly in place. Keep warm.

5 Just before you before you're ready to cook, place the wood chips or chunks on the coals, and oil the hot grates. Grill the steak, covered, for about 5 minutes per side for medium rare. Serve with the warm steak sauce.

BREAKOUT RECIPES
BURGERS

What the bulk of us who grew up in the suburbs think when we hear "barbecue" is grilling anything, but typically it means burgers and hot dogs. We're pretty sure you can do just fine grilling hot dogs, but we would be remiss if we didn't touch on the joy of the burger.

No. 9 BURGER

3 pounds ground beef (your favorite blend—ours is a sirloin-hanger blend with a 80:20 lean-to-fat ratio)

Salt and ground black pepper

6 large eggs

6 rolls

6 slices American cheese

12 slices cooked bacon

1 Preheat your grill to medium-high heat. Shape six 8-ounce burgers and season them liberally with salt and pepper. When the grill is hot, oil the grate and place the burgers on the grill. Cook for 3 to 5 minutes per side for rare—or longer if you want it more done.

2 While the burgers are cooking, fry the eggs sunny side up.

3 To assemble, place each burger on the bottom half of a roll, followed by a slice of cheese, 2 slices of bacon, and a fried egg. Cover it with the top half of the roll, grab a few extra napkins, and dig in.

MAKES 6 burgers

BBQ BURGER

3 pounds ground beef (your favorite blend—ours is a sirloin-hanger blend with a 80:20 lean-to-fat ratio)

Salt and ground black pepper

Brother Jimmy's Chipotle BBQ Sauce (page 33) for basting

6 slices cheddar cheese

6 rolls

Fried onions (page 107)

1 Preheat your grill to medium-high heat.

2 Shape six 8-ounce burgers and season them liberally with salt and pepper. When the grill is hot, oil the grate and place the burgers on the grill. Sear on each side.

3 Baste with the Chipotle BBQ Sauce. After about 3 to 5 minutes (for rare), place the cheese on to melt.

4 To assemble, place a burger on the bottom half of a roll, top with half of the fried onions, and then the top of the roll. Serve with the extra fried onions.

MAKES 6 burgers

BBQ BURGER

CHAPTER 8

POULTRY

SUPER BOWL SUNDAY

IS ESSENTIALLY A NATIONAL HOLIDAY. IT TICKS

off all the requisite boxes for any other recognized holiday: a large crew of friends and family (including some you rarely see), festive decorations (gotta have your team's colors displayed proudly, right?), enough beer and liquor to intoxicate a large army (if the fridge isn't overflowing, go buy more), some screaming and yelling (mostly at the TV; occasionally at a friend over a ruling on the field), and a table so overstocked with food that you worry about its structural integrity (and if you can fit just *one* more bowl of bean dip on there).

Not to mention that everyone laments about having to trudge into work the following day, grumbling that they should be allowed to turn up a little late. And you're still full the next day, if you've Super Bowled properly. That's because it's the second-largest day for food consumption in the United States, right after Thanksgiving Day. The only difference between the two festive affairs—because each is a football-themed day—is we swap out fowl types. Instead of slicing into a perfectly roasted (or deep-fried, if you're adventurous) turkey, we're pulling every last bit of meat off a succulent chicken wing.

In fact, if the reported stats are to be believed, as a nation, we're putting down about one billion chicken wings that Sunday. As far as beer consumption goes, we're draining 325 million gallons of brew into our stomachs, which is enough to fill about 500 Olympic-size swimming pools. So to say it's a party is a slight understatement. Surviving a Super Bowl fete is really a testament to gastrointestinal fortitude. Which means that you should feel extremely fortunate if you're not one of the people who are contributing to the 20 percent bump in antacid sales on Monday.

After all, when else is entirely overindulging on fried wings wholly acceptable and even encouraged? At Brother Jimmy's, during the pinnacle event of football season, we're doing our part to contribute to the wings and beer love-fest that overtakes our country. We're packed to the rafters and walls with super fans, slapping one another an abundance of high-fives whenever the pigskin advances. Given all the feverish activity, our patrons need to be fed more than adequately to keep them energized throughout the game. We're talking about serving quantities measured not by the plate, but by the bucket. Doesn't a bucket of anything always taste better?

SINCE POULTRY IS SUCH A VERSATILE PROTEIN, IT TAKES ON FLAVOR EASILY, SO YOU CAN APPEAL to anyone's palate, whether it is inherently geared toward savory, sweet, or spicy.

Super Bowl Sunday is far and away our biggest day for wing production at Brother Jimmy's. We deliver more containers of wings and have more orders placed for pickup than you can imagine. If we piled all the wings together—all 35,000—it'd take you a year to eat them, if you ate ninety-five wings per day. Speaking of piling, people start streaming through our doors around 3 P.M. and don't clear out until 11 P.M. Unless, of course, their team wins. In that case, they stay and party through the night. It usually holds true that the anticipation of the event is bigger than the actual game itself, so planning and preparation is vital.

We think poultry is the perfect accompaniment to this de facto holiday because no matter how it's prepared—be it baked, fried, stuffed, roasted, blackened, grilled, or pulled—it's simple to make it perfectly moist and tender. As an added bonus, if your poultry is served while it's still on the bone, you have a handy wand to wave frantically at the TV as you cheer and holler.

Since poultry is such a versatile protein, it takes on flavor easily, so you can appeal to anyone's palate, whether it is inherently geared toward savory, sweet, or spicy. Chicken does particularly well with a brine, and our Garlic, Jalapeño, and Lime–Brined Chicken is proof of that. The flavors are so engrained within the chicken breast that even a serious dunking in water to get all the peppercorns off has absolutely no effect on the flavor that explodes with every bite after coming off the grill. It's so unbelievably great that people won't mind missing the game for a bit while they're queuing up for thirds and fourths.

We've also got some unique methods of cooking, which will be sure to dazzle even the most stoic of your guests (like the Deep-Fried Cajun Chicken, in which you plunk a liberally seasoned whole chicken into a vat of bubbling oil). It's all pretty basic kitchen stuff, which means you get to spend the maximum amount of time celebrating with your guests, yet you're not skimping on the maximum taste.

If you're hosting a Super Bowl bash, you're nearly obligated to make sure the food spread for your grazing friends is copious enough to easily feed one of the competing gridiron teams. And because eating contests are popular at Super Bowl parties—particularly during commercial breaks and at halftime—there's no reason you can't have a fried chicken face-off in your own home with each of your guests entering his or her best recipe and collectively voting to decide who takes home the Super Bucket trophy. And you best have a laughable trophy handy, or a decent cash prize—people have to pay back their bookies somehow.

PLAYLIST

It's Super Bowl! A time for manliness. And then some more manliness. These testosterone-laden songs are sure you get you all psyched up for the big game. Make sure you have ample room to play air guitar with these tracks. If your home will allow it, we also encourage the rocker power slide. For the uninitiated, this is where you run, then drop to your knees and slide, coming to rest in the middle of the room, all the while belting out the lyrics. It's what all the cool kids are doing.

HANK WILLIAMS, JR.
ARE YOU READY FOR SOME FOOTBALL?!

JAY-Z
RUN THIS TOWN

JOAN JETT AND THE BLACKHEARTS
I LOVE ROCK 'N' ROLL

AC/DC
BACK IN BLACK

VAN HALEN
AND THE CRADLE WILL ROCK

BON JOVI
IT'S MY LIFE

BLACK EYED PEAS
I GOTTA FEELING

MICHAEL FRANTI
SAY HEY (I LOVE YOU)

LUCKY BOYS CONFUSION
BOSSMAN

KINGS OF LEON
THE BUCKET

TODD RUNDGREN
BANG THE DRUM ALL DAY

THE RAMONES
BLITZKRIEG BOP

RED HOT CHILI PEPPERS
GIVE IT AWAY

KID ROCK
COWBOY

JANE'S ADDICTION
STOP

BLACK SABBATH
PARANOID

GUNS N' ROSES
PARADISE CITY

GREEN DAY
LONGVIEW

PEARL JAM
WORLD WIDE SUICIDE

FOO FIGHTERS
THE PRETENDER

SOUTHERN FRIED CHICKEN
WITH TOASTED GARLIC

6 garlic cloves, finely chopped

2 cups all-purpose flour

1 tablespoon kosher salt

1 tablespoon ground
black pepper

¼ teaspoon ground
white pepper

1½ teaspoons granulated garlic

2 large eggs

1 cup evaporated milk

1 teaspoon Frank's Red Hot
Sauce (optional)

1 (3-pound) fryer chicken,
cut into 8 pieces

2 to 3 cups canola oil for frying

SERVES 4 to 6

Who doesn't love crispy deep-fried chicken, bursting with juices at first bite? We've added toasted garlic for a little more depth of flavor.

1 Preheat the oven to 300°F. Lay parchment paper on a baking sheet and sprinkle the garlic on top, dispersing it as much as possible. Place in the oven and bake for about 30 minutes, moving the garlic around every 10 minutes or so, until golden brown and crisp. Cool and crush the garlic slightly with the bottom of a sauté pan to break it up.

2 Combine the flour, salt, black pepper, white pepper, and granulated garlic in a shallow bowl. In a separate shallow bowl, beat the eggs with the evaporated milk and add the hot sauce.

3 Pat the chicken pieces dry and dredge them in the flour, shaking off as much excess as you can. Place in the egg mixture, then back into the flour coating. Make sure there are no wet patches on the chicken or the coating will not stay on.

4 Start by heating 2 cups of the oil in a heavy flat-bottomed pan (cast iron is ideal) over medium-high heat. The oil should be about halfway up the side of the chicken—if it isn't, add more oil. When the oil is hot but not smoking, start frying. (It should crackle if you drop a bit of flour into it.) If you don't have a big enough pan to cook all of the chicken at once, then do it in batches, starting with the legs and thighs, which take the longest, 15 to 20 minutes.

5 Turn the chicken often to ensure even cooking and coloring. When the chicken is done, place it on a platter and sprinkle the toasted garlic on top. You can keep the chicken warm in a 300°F oven if you're making it in batches.

FRIED CHICKEN BREASTS

1 cup all-purpose flour

1½ teaspoons kosher salt

½ teaspoon ground black pepper

1 large egg

½ cup buttermilk

1 cup canola oil for frying

3 to 4 boneless, skinless chicken breasts, trimmed of any fat

SERVES 3 to 4

This is the base for all of our recipes that include fried chicken. It's a simple, easy, and delicious staple you'll use more than you think. If you want to get creative, you can experiment with adding various spices and herbs to the flour mixture. For Buffalo Fried Chicken Breasts, just toss the finished cooked chicken in Buffalo Sauce (page 36) to coat.

1 In a shallow bowl, combine the flour, salt, and pepper. In a separate shallow bowl, beat the egg with the buttermilk.

2 Heat the oil over medium heat in a large frying pan.

3 Dredge the chicken in the flour, then into the egg mixture, then back into the flour.

4 When the oil is hot, place the chicken in the pan. Cook for 10 to 15 minutes until golden brown, turning a few times to cook evenly.

BUFFALO CHICKEN SANDWICH

With the classic Buffalo chicken wing combo in every bite, this sandwich is quick and simple to make and never disappoints eager mouths.

2 batches Fried Chicken Breasts (above)

Buffalo Sauce (page 36)

6 sandwich rolls

Blue Cheese Dressing (page 36)

¼ to ½ head iceberg lettuce, shredded

SERVES 6

1 Prepare the Fried Chicken Breasts, then toss in the Buffalo Sauce to coat it well.

2 Slice the rolls and place a Fried Chicken Breast on the bottom of each one. On top of the chicken, place a nice dollop of the Blue Cheese Dressing, followed by some of the shredded lettuce. Top with the top half of the roll.

TURKEY
BURGER
WITH CHIPOTLE BBQ MAYO

A turkey burger can taste just as delicious as a ground beef burger, and it's a healthier option. The potato rolls are the perfect resting place for these patties.

1 **Make the Chipotle BBQ Mayo:** In a medium bowl, whisk all the ingredients together until well incorporated. Cover and refrigerate until ready to use.

2 **Make the burgers:** In a large bowl, combine all the ingredients and mix well. Form 6 equal-size burgers, no more than ½ inch thick.

3 Cook on a well-oiled griddle pan or frying pan over medium-low heat for 4 to 5 minutes per side. Cover once the burgers are added to the pan, and then again after you flip them because this will help retain moisture.

4 Place inside a roll and top with the Chipotle BBQ Mayo.

FOR THE CHIPOTLE BBQ MAYO:

½ cup Hellman's mayonnaise

¼ cup Brother Jimmy's Chipotle BBQ Sauce (page 33)

¼ teaspoon Chipotle Puree (page 32)

¼ teaspoon kosher salt

FOR THE BURGERS:

2 pounds ground turkey (we prefer the leg/thigh)

3 tablespoons ketchup

1½ tablespoons Worcestershire sauce

1½ teaspoons dried oregano

1½ teaspoons salt

¾ teaspoon granulated garlic

¼ teaspoon ground black pepper

★

6 potato rolls

SERVES 6

BBQ CHICKEN

Brining the poultry helps make this barbecue staple extra-flavorful as well as extra-moist. Most people will want seconds, so just multiply the recipe by the number of birds you want to serve.

1 **Make the brine:** Place 1 cup of the water in a small saucepan over low heat and add the sugar, salt, and chile powder. Cook until the sugar and salt dissolve. Remove from the heat and add the juice or cider and the remaining water. Refrigerate until it is cold.

2 Place the chicken into the cold brine—either in a brining bag, a large zip-top bag, or a bowl—and refrigerate from 8 hours to overnight. About 20 minutes before you're ready to grill, pull the chicken out of the refrigerator and let come to room temperature.

3 Prepare your smoker or grill for barbecuing, using the indirect heat setup (see page 15) with a drip pan in place, and preheat to 240°F. Have 3 or 4 wood chunks soaking and ready to go (we recommend apple). Just before you're ready to cook, pour some water in the drip pan and place the wood on the hot coals.

4 Remove the chicken from the brine and pat dry. Smoke for about 3 hours, covered, until the chicken reaches an internal temperature of 170°F when tested at the thigh joint. This could take from 3 to 5 hours, depending on your equipment.

5 Finish the chicken on the grill over direct, medium-high heat, basting it with the BBQ Sauce and letting the sauce caramelize.

FOR THE BRINE:

3 cups cold water

¼ cup sugar

7 teaspoons kosher salt

2¼ teaspoons ancho chile powder

1 cup apple juice or cider

1 (3½- to 4-pound) chicken, cut in half

1 cup Brother Jimmy's Original BBQ Sauce (page 31)

SERVES 4

PULLED CHICKEN

6 pounds chicken legs

Salt and ground black pepper

½ to ¾ cup Brother Jimmy's Original BBQ Sauce (page 31)

SERVES 6

Pulled chicken is a perfect filling and topping for sandwiches, quesadillas, grilled pizzas, nachos, and more. The possibilities are endless with this versatile recipe.

1 Lightly season the chicken legs with salt and pepper.

2 Prepare your smoker or grill for barbecuing, using the indirect heat setup (see page 15) with a drip pan in place, and preheat to between 225°F and 240°F. Have 3 or 4 wood chunks soaking and ready to go.

3 Just before you're ready to cook, pour some water in the drip pan, place the presoaked wood chunks on the hot coals, and oil the hot grate. Smoke the chicken for about 4 hours, until an internal temperature of 180°F is reached at the joint.

4 When the chicken is ready, place it in a bowl and let it cool until you are able to handle it.

5 Pull the skin off and discard it. Then pull the meat off the bones, breaking up the larger pieces.

6 Mix with the BBQ Sauce, adjusting the amount to your liking.

PULLED CHICKEN WRAP
WITH BACON & CHEDDAR

This is a great use for leftover pulled chicken. We've given quantities based on one wrap, so multiply by the number of people you want to feed.

1 (12-inch) flour tortilla

2 slices cheddar cheese

¾ cup hot Pulled Chicken (page 164)

2 slices cooked bacon

SERVES 1

1 Keep the tortilla at room temperature for easier rolling or warm it in the oven for 1 minute.

2 Place the cheese slices, side by side, just below the center of the tortilla, leaving about 1½ inches on either side. Place the pulled chicken on top of the cheese and then add the bacon.

3 Fold the bottom part of the tortilla up over the filling, tuck it in toward the filling, then fold the sides in. Start to roll toward the top until the tortilla is wrapped all around.

4 Cut in half and serve.

BREAKOUT RECIPES

CHICKEN WINGS

These little morsels of tastiness are like tiny canvases; they'll take any flavor or method of cooking. How you choose to adorn them is up to you, but we've got a few suggestions that have always been a hit at our restaurants. Make sure you have plenty of napkins on hand because a wing feast can get pretty messy rather quickly—especially with those who are sauce fanatics. And also have a garbage bag ready for all the discarded bones. It's never a pretty sight to pile them on a plate.

TEQUILA-LIME WINGS

4 pounds chicken wings

FOR THE TEQUILA-LIME MARINADE:

½ cup tequila

Zest and juice of 2 limes

1 jalapeño, seeded and very thinly sliced

1 tablespoon kosher salt

1 teaspoon ground black pepper

¼ cup canola oil

1 Cut the pointy tips off the chicken wings, and either discard or save for chicken stock. Cut the wing in half at the joint.

2 In a gallon-size zip-top bag, combine the ingredients for the marinade. Give it a little swish to mix and add the wings. Marinate in the refrigerator for 4 to 6 hours or up to overnight.

About 15 minutes before you're ready to grill, pull the wings out of the refrigerator and let come to room temperature.

3 When you are ready to cook the wings, preheat your grill to moderate heat.

4 Oil the hot grate and place the wings on the grill. Do not discard the marinade. Cook the wings for 12 to 18 minutes, depending on the size of the wings, until done; they should reached an internal temperature of 165°F at the joint bone.

5 While the wings are cooking, pour the marinade into a small saucepan and bring to a boil. Lower the heat and simmer for about 10 minutes, until it thickens.

6 Place the cooked wings into a bowl and toss with the reduced marinade, which is now a glaze.

SERVES 6 to 8

BUFFALO WINGS

CHIPOTLE WINGS

TEQUILA-LIME WINGS

JERKED WINGS

4 pounds chicken wings

FOR THE JERK MARINADE:

2 tablespoons dried thyme

4 scallions, cut into 2-inch pieces

¼ cup ground allspice

1 teaspoon ground nutmeg

1 teaspoon ground cinnamon

1 to 5 ounces habañero sauce (we like Melinda's Habanero Hot Sauce)

½ cup soy sauce

2 tablespoons finely grated fresh ginger

½ cup diced onion

3 garlic cloves

Zest and juice of 3 limes

½ cup packed brown sugar

· ·

1 Cut the pointy tips off the chicken wings, and either discard or save for chicken stock. Cut the wing in half at the joint.

2 Combine all the ingredients for the marinade in a blender and blend until the scallions are well chopped.

3 Place half of the marinade in a gallon-size zip-top bag (reserve the other half for basting). Add the wings to the bag, seal it, and shake to coat the wings. Set in the refrigerator and marinate for 6 to 8 hours or up to overnight. About 15 minutes before you're ready to grill, pull the wings out of the refrigerator and let come to room temperature.

4 Preheat your grill to moderate heat. Oil the hot grate and grill the wings, turning often and basting them with the reserved jerk sauce. Cook the wings for 12 to 18 minutes, or until they reach an internal temperature of 165°F at the bone joint.

SERVES 6 to 8

TERIYAKI WINGS

FOR THE TERIYAKI SAUCE:

¼ cup low-sodium soy sauce

¼ cup brown sugar

2 tablespoons minced or finely grated fresh ginger

5 garlic cloves, minced or grated

¾ teaspoon crushed red pepper flakes

¼ cup ketchup

½ cup hoisin sauce

2 tablespoons rice vinegar

 ★

About 4 cups canola oil for deep-frying

3 to 4 pounds chicken wings

2 scallions, very thinly sliced

1 teaspoon sesame seeds

· ·

1 Cut the pointy tips off the chicken wings, and either discard or save for chicken stock. Cut the wing in half at the joint.

2 **Make the sauce:** Combine the ingredients for the sauce in a saucepan, place over medium heat, bring to a simmer, and cook until slightly thickened, about 10 minutes. Set aside.

3 While the sauce is cooking, heat 5 to 6 inches of oil in a deep-fryer or heavy-bottomed stockpot to 350°F. Place the wings into the hot oil and cook until golden and crisp, about 12 to 15 minutes. Depending on the size of your pot, you may need to do this in two batches.

4 Using the deep-fryer's wire basket, a slotted spoon, or a spider, remove the wings and drain for a moment on paper towels or on a wire rack. When all the wings are cooked, toss them in a bowl with about half of the sauce, the scallions, and sesame seeds.

5 Use the reserved sauce for extra dipping.

SERVES 6 to 8

BUFFALO WINGS

4 pounds chicken wings

2¼ teaspoons salt

1½ teaspoons white pepper

1½ teaspoons chili powder

1⅛ teaspoons paprika

⅛ teaspoon granulated garlic

About 8 cups canola oil for deep-frying, plus 1 tablespoon for coating the wings

½ cup Buffalo Sauce (page 36) for serving

2 cups Blue Cheese Dressing (page 36) for serving

Celery sticks for serving

1 Cut the pointy tips off the chicken wings, and either discard or save for chicken stock. Then cut the wing in half at the joint.

2 In a large bowl, combine the salt, white pepper, chili powder, paprika, and granulated garlic. Add the wings and the 1 tablespoon of oil. Toss together to coat the wings. Cover and marinate in the refrigerator for 1 to 2 hours. About 15 minutes before you're ready to bake the wings, pull them out of the refrigerator and let come to room temperature.

3 Preheat the oven to 350°F. Lay the seasoned wings on a sheet pan and bake for 15 minutes.

4 Cool the wings completely. (You may do steps 1 through 3 a day earlier, if you like. The wings will keep for 2 to 3 days in the fridge.)

5 Heat 5 to 6 inches of oil in a deep-fryer or heavy-bottomed stockpot to 350°F. Place the wings into the hot oil and cook until crisp, 7 to 9 minutes. Depending on the size of your pot, you may need to do this in two batches.

6 Using the deep-fryer's wire basket, a slotted spoon, or a spider, remove to a bowl and toss with the Buffalo Sauce.

7 Serve with the Blue Cheese Dressing and celery sticks.

SERVES 6 to 8

MAPLE BBQ WINGS

4 pounds chicken wings

1 tablespoon Southern Rub (page 26)

¾ cup maple syrup

1 teaspoon chili powder

½ teaspoon ground coriander

1 teaspoon dry mustard

¼ teaspoon ground black pepper

1 teaspoon lemon zest

2 tablespoons lemon juice

2 tablespoons brown sugar

¼ cup water

1 tablespoon Worcestershire sauce

1 tablespoon bourbon

1 tablespoon Dijon mustard

1 Cut the pointy tips off the chicken wings, and either discard or save for chicken stock. Cut the wing in half at the joint.

2 Prepare your smoker or grill for barbecuing, using the indirect heat setup (see page 15) with a drip pan in place, and preheat to 220°F. Have applewood or cherrywood chunks or wood chips soaking and ready to go.

3 Just before you're ready to cook, place the presoaked wood chunks (or a packet of presoaked wood chips) directly on the hot coals and oil the hot grate. Smoke the wings, covered, for about 2 hours, until an internal temperature of 165°F at a joint bone has been reached.

4 Place all the ingredients for the sauce in a medium nonreactive saucepan, place over medium heat, bring to a simmer, and cook for about 20 minutes, until sauce thickens.

5 Preheat your grill to moderate heat. Oil the hot grate; place the smoked wings on the grill and baste with the sauce. You'll want the sauce to caramelize in a couple of additions, so take them off occasionally and give them a quick toss in a bowl with the sauce. Be careful not to burn them, as there is a lot of sugar in the sauce, and sugar cooks quickly.

SERVES 6 to 8

CHIPOTLE WINGS

4 pounds chicken wings

1 tablespoon Southern Rub (page 26)

½ cup Brother Jimmy's Chipotle BBQ Sauce (page 33)

1 Cut the pointy tips off the chicken wings, and either discard or save for chicken stock. Cut the wing in half at the joint.

2 Prepare your smoker or grill for barbecuing, using the indirect heat setup (see page 15) with a drip pan in place, and preheat to 220°F. Have applewood or cherrywood chunks or wood chips soaking and ready to go.

3 Just before you're ready to cook, place the presoaked wood chunks (or a packet of presoaked wood chips) directly on the hot coals and oil the hot grate. Smoke the wings, covered, for about 2 hours, until an internal temperature of 165°F at a joint bone has been reached.

4 Place the smoked wings in a bowl and toss with half of the Chipotle BBQ Sauce.

5 Preheat your grill to moderate heat. Oil the hot grate and place the wings on the grill to caramelize the sauce. When you are ready to turn the wings, place them back in the bowl, toss with the remaining sauce, and return them to the grill.

6 When the sauce seems like it's cooked onto the wings, they're done; this will take 5 to 6 minutes.

SERVES 6 to 8

DRINKS: TRY THESE LIBATIONS at your next Super Bowl bash:

BATTLE OF ANTIETAM BLOODY MARY

You'll likely be starting the celebrating early, so there's no better time to have a Bloody Mary. Our twist on the classic cocktail includes our special rimming spice— salt, celery seed, and Old Bay—and a festive array of garnishes. See the recipe on page 68.

BLOODY BEER

If you're of the mind-set that 12 P.M. is too early for vodka, how about beer? Our Bloody Beer mixes Budweiser, tomato juice, Tabasco Sauce, Worcestershire sauce, and fresh lime, and it goes down smooth every time. See the recipe on page 67.

BEER

As you might have noticed from this book, beer goes with everything. So yeah. Buy some more beer.

DRUNKEN SAILOR

This one's always a hit among the ladies 'round my pen. It's spiced rum and Cheerwine. If you don't have Cheerwine handy, substitute some Cherry Coke. See the recipe on page 60.

DEEP-FRIED
CAJUN CHICKEN

1 (3½- to 4-pound) chicken

¼ cup store-bought Cajun spice (we recommend Paul Prudhomme's Cajun Magic)

2 to 3 gallons canola oil, as needed

FOR THE INJECTION:

¼ cup lemon juice

¼ cup beer

¼ cup olive oil or melted unsalted butter

2 tablespoons Cajun spice

SPECIAL EQUIPMENT:

A turkey fryer (don't fill the oil level more than halfway up the pot to prevent boiling over)

A kitchen syringe

A deep-fat-fryer thermometer

SERVES 2 to 4

For this simple yet potentially dangerous recipe, we recommend using a turkey fryer—a large pot with a device to lower and raise the turkey or chicken from the oil—as it is a safer way to deep-fry a bird. Make sure to follow the manufacturer's directions for safe frying and trussing the chicken. Take serious care when lowering the chicken into the hot oil. ("See Deep-Frying 101" on page 77 if you're a first-time fryer.)

1 Rub the chicken inside and out with the Cajun spice, cover, and refrigerate from 6 hours to overnight. About 30 minutes before you're ready to fry, pull the chicken out of the refrigerator and let come to room temperature.

2 In a medium bowl, combine the ingredients for the injection. Pull as much of the liquid as you can through a syringe and inject all parts of the chicken several times.

3 Heat the oil in a turkey fryer until it reads 350°F on a deep-fat-fryer thermometer.

4 When you are ready to lower the chicken, do it very slowly, inch by inch, with the trussed legs up. If you do it too quickly, the oil could shoot up through the cavity of the chicken. Fry for about 20 minutes, until the internal temperature—taken at the thigh joint—is 155°F.

5 Slowly lift the chicken out of the oil, making sure to let the majority of the excess oil drip back into the pot. Transfer the chicken to a counter and let it rest for 10 minutes before carving into it.

HONEY-BRINED

TURKEY BREAST

This is perfect sliced up and served over some mashed potatoes (or by itself), or it can be saved to make the ideal turkey sandwich.

1 Combine ¾ cup of the water in a medium saucepan with the honey, brown sugar, salt, garlic, peppercorns, mustard seeds, allspice, and cloves. Place over medium heat and cook, whisking, until the honey, salt, and brown sugar dissolve.

2 Remove from the heat and pour into a large nonreactive container. Add the remaining water. Cool in the refrigerator completely before putting the turkey in.

3 Remove any netting from the turkey and place in the brine—weigh it down with small plates—and refrigerate overnight. About 30 minutes before you're ready to grill, pull the turkey breast out of the refrigerator and let come to room temperature.

4 Prepare your smoker or grill for barbecuing, using the indirect heat setup (see page 15) with a drip pan in place, and preheat to 225°F. Have a packet of presoaked wood chips or chunks at the ready. When you're ready to cook, pour some water in the drip pan, place the wood chips or chunks directly on the hot coals, and oil the hot grate. Smoke the turkey breast until the internal temperature reaches 150°F. Remove it and wrap it in foil to retain moisture and to allow the carryover cooking to occur without drying out.

FOR THE BRINE:

2¾ cups cold water

1 cup honey

½ cup brown sugar

¾ cup salt

¼ cup garlic cloves

1 tablespoon whole black peppercorns

1 tablespoon mustard seeds

2 allspice berries

2 whole cloves

★

1 (2½-pound) boneless turkey breast

SERVES 6

GARLIC, JALAPEÑO &
LIME-BRINED CHICKEN
WITH RAINBOW SLAW

Brining keeps the chicken moist and succulent, and the flavor of the jalapeño comes through without a burning heat finish. The rainbow slaw is the perfect crunchy and cool complement to the warm, tender chicken.

1 Make the brine: Combine 2 cups of the water, the salt, sugar, garlic, lime zest, jalapeños, and peppercorns in a saucepan, place over medium heat, and heat until the sugar and salt dissolve, about 5 to 8 minutes. Remove from the heat, add the remaining 4 cups of water, cover, and refrigerate until cold.

2 Add the chicken to the cold brine, cover, and refrigerate for 8 hours or up to overnight.

3 About an hour before you're ready cook the chicken, prepare the Rainbow Slaw (it needs to sit for the flavors to meld).

4 Preheat your grill to medium heat and, about 15 minutes before you're ready to grill, pull the chicken out of the refrigerator and let come to room temperature.

5 Oil the hot grate and grill the chicken for 5 to 8 minutes per side, until cooked through. Brined foods tend to cook more quickly, so be careful not to overcook.

6 Place the slaw on a platter. Slice the chicken and serve alongside or on top of the slaw.

FOR THE BRINE:

6 cups cold water

¼ cup salt

½ cup sugar

⅓ cup garlic cloves

Zest of 3 limes

1 jalapeño, sliced

1 tablespoon whole black peppercorns, crushed a little with the back of a pan

6 boneless, skinless chicken breasts, lightly pounded to even them out

1 recipe Rainbow Slaw (page 48)

SERVES 6

MOM'S BBQ

CHUNKY PEANUT BUTTER CHICKEN

This is one of those dishes that's perfect for summer because it's great hot or cold. It makes a mess of the grill, but the flavor makes the cleanup entirely worth it.

FOR THE MARINADE:

1½ tablespoons chopped garlic

2 tablespoons minced or finely grated ginger

2 tablespoons soy sauce

1 cup peanut butter (the chunkier, the better)

1 (6-ounce) can pineapple juice

2 tablespoons honey

1½ teaspoons salt

4 to 5 pounds chicken parts

SERVES 8

1 Combine all the ingredients for the marinade in a large bowl and whisk to incorporate the peanut butter and honey. Add the chicken and toss to evenly coat; let it sit for 15 minutes.

2 Preheat your grill to moderate heat and oil the grates well.

3 Cook the chicken, turning often so it doesn't burn. Grill for 20 to 30 minutes, until it reaches an internal temperature of 165ºF at the joint bone.

SUPERFLUOUS SUPER BOWL DRINKING GAMES:

I HEART ANY GAME THAT USES A PIGSKIN, provided it's actually not made from the skin or bladder of a pig. There's a ton of fun drinking (and nondrinking) games you can play during the Super Bowl to help ensure you're capitalizing on all the fun that can be had. And maximizing your beer intake. These little numbers should get you and your friends well on your way in no time flat.

SCORING DRINKING GAME

Throughout the game, take one sip for every touchdown by your team and two sips every time the opponent scores. Or you can assign a drink value to scored points, too, so three sips for a field goal, seven sips on the touchdowns.

KEYWORD DRINKING GAME

This one is a little more fun. Before the game, have everyone write down one or two words or phrases you think you'll hear often during game play. Assign each a drink value. So for instance, you'll drink once every time you hear the word "flag" and twice whenever a player says "it is what it is." Be as creative as possible. I recommend the following: "fumble," "just shy of," "what a hit," "deep in the pocket," and any mention of "Brett Favre." If you want to get super-serious, up the level of difficulty with gems like "sexual harassment suit," "arrested," "like a rock" (applicable only during truck commercials), or any mention of "beer." Careful with the last one; that has the potential to get you soused quick.

PICK-A-PLAYER

Jot down the names of the key players in the game on both teams. Drop them all in a bowl and have everyone draw a name. Each time that player is remotely involved with a play, that friend gets to pass out one drink to whomever he or she chooses. Just don't haze the new guy or girl too much, okay? It's up to you whether or not to include quarterbacks—and it really depends on how drunk you wish to become. Finally, if your player happens to score a touchdown, that's seven drinks for you.

PASS THE CUP

This one's simple and can be altered for gambling purposes. The only requisite is that all players should be drinking the same brand of beer. One person starts by putting a splash of beer into a cup and naming a play, like first down or field goal. For each play that is not the one named, each person quickly pours a bit of beer in the cup and passes it on. When the play finally occurs, the person holding the cup drinks the whole thing. You can substitute one-dollar bills for pours of beer to make the game more lucrative.

THANKSGIVING

PULLED TURKEY

WITH CRANBERRY BBQ SAUCE

FOR THE BRINE:

1 gallon cold water

1 cup salt

1 cup brown sugar

1 cup honey

3 tablespoons whole black peppercorns

1 cup garlic cloves

4 allspice berries

3 tablespoons mustard seeds

1 tablespoon rubbed sage leaves

★

6 turkey legs

FOR THE CRANBERRY BBQ SAUCE:

1 pound fresh cranberries

1 jalapeño

1 cup water

1¼ to 1½ cups sugar

½ cup diced red onion

2 tablespoons red wine vinegar

1½ teaspoons salt

¾ teaspoon orange zest

SERVES 6

This isn't your mom's Thanksgiving turkey. Flavored with a sweet and tangy brine, it's great sliced and eaten straight up on the plate or in a sandwich or wrap. The recipe for the Cranberry BBQ Sauce will be more than you need for this amount of turkey legs, but it's so good, you may just want to double the amount of turkey legs you smoke. The leftover bones also add great flavor when cooking beans or soup.

1 **Make the brine:** Combine ½ gallon (8 cups) of the water with the salt, brown sugar, honey, black peppercorns, garlic cloves, allspice, mustard seeds, and sage in a large saucepan. Bring to a simmer and cook until the salt, brown sugar, and honey dissolve.

2 Remove from the heat and pour onto a container large enough to hold the brine and the turkey legs. Add the remaining cold water and let cool to 40°F in the refrigerator before adding the turkey legs.

3 Brine the legs from 8 hours to overnight in the refrigerator. About 20 minutes before you're ready to grill, pull the turkey legs out of the refrigerator and let come to room temperature.

4 Prepare your smoker or grill for barbecuing, using the indirect heat setup (see page 15) with a drip pan and a packet of wood chips or chunks in place, and preheat to 220°F. Just before you're ready to cook, pour some water in the drip pan and oil the hot grate. Rinse off the brine and smoke for 4 to 6 hours, until an internal temperature of 185°F is reached. Let cool slightly. (Be sure to use a water pan to keep the moisture level up, because there isn't much fat in the legs.)

5 **Make the BBQ sauce:** While the meat is cooling, combine all the ingredients in a nonreactive 2-quart saucepan. Place over medium-high heat, bring to a boil, then reduce the heat and simmer for 25 minutes. Cool, transfer to a blender, and blend until smooth.

6 Pull the turkey off the bone into a bowl, making sure to remove all the tendons, grizzle, and fat. Mix the turkey meat with enough of the Cranberry BBQ Sauce to evenly and lightly coat.

CITRUS-GRILLED
CHICKEN LEGS & THIGHS

The bright citrus flavors from the zest make this chicken taste like summer exploded in your mouth. The citrus holds up well against the fatty content of the legs and thighs.

FOR THE THREE-CITRUS MARINADE:

3 garlic cloves, minced or finely grated

Zest and juice of 1 orange

Zest of 2 limes

Juice of 1 lime

Zest of 2 lemons

1 tablespoon salt

½ teaspoon ground black pepper

¼ cup olive oil

★

8 chicken legs and thighs

SERVES 6 to 8

1 Combine all the ingredients for the marinade in a large nonreactive bowl or large zip-top bag. Add the chicken pieces and toss or shake to evenly coat; cover or seal and marinate in the refrigerator for 2 to 4 hours.

2 About 15 minutes before you're ready to grill, pull the chicken pieces out of the refrigerator and let come to room temperature.

3 Preheat your grill to moderate heat. Have some wood chunks or chips soaking and ready to throw on.

4 Just before you before you're ready to cook, oil the hot grates. Grill the chicken for 20 to 30 minutes, covered, until cooked through.

BLACKENED
CHICKEN

This is another one of our staple recipes. It is great with Smoky Corn and Black Bean Chow Chow (page 212) on the side or cut up atop a salad. Remember that "blackened" doesn't mean "burned," folks.

2 tablespoons Blackening Spice (page 29)

6 boneless, skinless chicken breasts, trimmed of excess fat or sinew

4 to 6 tablespoons vegetable oil

Salt

SERVES 6

1 Sprinkle the Blackening Spice on the smooth side of the chicken breasts.

2 Heat a cast-iron pan over medium-high heat until very hot, add the oil, then place the chicken in the pan spice-side down. Sprinkle with salt and lower the heat to medium.

3 Cook for 4 to 5 minutes, then turn the breast over, cover the pan to keep some moisture in, and cook for another 4 to 5 minutes, until cooked through.

FRIED CHICKEN & WAFFLES

1¾ cups all-purpose flour

1¼ cups cornmeal

1 tablespoon baking powder

1 teaspoon sugar

1 teaspoon salt

2 cups milk

3 tablespoons vegetable oil (or any flavorless oil)

2 large eggs

Cooking spray

4 Fried Chicken Breasts (page 160)

Maple syrup

SERVES 4

Another Southern tradition, the sauce for this dish can change regionally, but we like it with a good dose of maple syrup. And don't think you're limited to serving it for dinner; it's popular at brunch in our restaurants.

1 Combine the flour, cornmeal, baking powder, sugar, and salt in a large bowl.

2 In a separate bowl, whisk together the milk, oil, and eggs.

3 Add the wet mixture to the dry mixture and mix until smooth.

4 Heat a Belgian-style waffle iron and spray with cooking spray. Cook the waffles according to the manufacturer's instructions.

5 Serve with the Fried Chicken Breasts on top of the waffle and maple syrup on the side.

CHAPTER 9

SEAFOOD

UP UNTIL NOW, WE'VE

BEEN TALKING ABOUT ALL TYPES OF BARBECUES

involving all sorts of beef, pork, and fowl. But we're not overlooking the fruits of the sea. On coastal towns nestled on the shores of America, the clambake or boil is the euphemism for the barbecue, because fish and an abundance of other tasty seafood are within a pole's or net's reach. Sure, the period of nice weather is shorter in some of the more northern regions, which makes the clambake that much more of an inherent party. It's a little tough to have a festive lobster bake in Maine in the middle of January.

In the South, however, boils are happening year-round. A boil is the seafood version of a pig pickin', and it's a general term used for large gatherings, typically involving massive consumption of shellfish cooked in a huge boiling pot. Southerners will tell you that any reason, no matter how flimsy, is a perfect occasion for a boil; they just love the celebratory aspect of the feast. Baby shower? Boil time. Wedding anniversary? Grab the pot. Cousin's got a new job? Let's do this. It's Saturday? Sure, that works, too.

Typically, there's not much meat tucked inside these little critters of the sea, so a boil ends up being a bit of hard work to get enough meat out to be filling. Because you're usually standing at a table rather than sitting, with claws and shells being cracked left and right, it's a messy meal. Boil guests who opt to skip a bib end up with a stained shirt quite often, but a proper boil host has a hose nearby so you can wash your hands off right after you're done chowing down. Because of all of this, the boil isn't so much about the food as it is about camaraderie, though you should always be serving some serious grub.

Even though we're not in Louisiana (boil country) every year for Fat Tuesday—and when the New Orleans Saints were making their run at a Super Bowl championship—at Brother Jimmy's restaurants we have crawfish boils, complete with potatoes and corn, seasoned to perfection. We happen to think there is no better way to pair food with booze than with a boil. Thanks to the salty water, the more you eat, the thirstier you get. Which is why we have extra beers waiting in our coolers.

Don't fret that the grill or your smoker is going to be left out of our dive into the realm of seafood. We've got scores of treats that don't involve a bubbling cauldron of clawed critters. Salmon, tuna, catfish, scallops, and lobster (including a killer lobster roll that'll convert any non–shellfish eater instantly) are all covered. You can even smoke some of the fish fillets right alongside other proteins, so your guests will have every genre of meat available. And all of our fish recipes have a bit of a Southern twist, whether it's through a smoked tomato *mojo* sauce for striped bass or a guava BBQ sauce for your salmon. There's no reason the South in your mouth can't have originated from the ocean.

PLAYLIST

Get yourself down to the bayou—at least mentally—and throw together a boil playlist. These selections of feel-good songs are the perfect complement to any backyard seafood extravaganza. Classic country, blues, and even a touch of reggae are sure to make you feel good and happy. Just be careful when manning your playing device if you're mid-boil—the juices from your food don't mix well with iPods or docks.

THE NEVILLE BROTHERS
LOVE THE ONE YOU'RE WITH

BILL WITHERS
USE ME

B. B. KING
PLAYING WITH MY FRIENDS

CLARENCE GATEMOUTH BROWN
MIDNITE HOUR

MUDDY WATERS
I CAN'T BE SATISFIED

ALABAMA
LOUISIANA SATURDAY NIGHT

HOT TUNA
HESITATION BLUES

STEVIE RAY VAUGHAN
PRIDE AND JOY

DR. JOHN
RIGHT PLACE WRONG TIME

UNCLE KRACKER
DRIFT AWAY

CREEDENCE CLEARWATER REVIVAL
BORN ON THE BAYOU

BOB DYLAN
ROLLIN' AND TUMBLIN'

BRUCE SPRINGSTEEN
OLD DAN TUCKER

THE BLUES BROTHERS
SHE CAUGHT THE KATY

COWBOY MOUTH
HOW DO YOU TELL SOMEONE

JIMMY BUFFETT
FINS

BOB MARLEY & THE WAILERS
STIR IT UP

JIMMY CLIFF
WONDERFUL WORLD, BEAUTIFUL PEOPLE

VAN MORRISON
BRIGHT SIDE OF THE ROAD

THE DOOBIE BROTHERS
BLACK WATER

PAUL SIMON
ME AND JULIO DOWN BY THE SCHOOLYARD

THE NEVILLE BROTHERS
CONGO SQUARE

CATFISH
PO' BOYS

We also make these sandwiches with Popcorn Shrimp (page 86) and Blackened Chicken (page 181). Whatever your po' boy filling, it's bound to be delicious.

1 Heat the oil in a large sauté pan (cast iron if you have it) over medium-high heat.

2 Sprinkle the Blackening Spice on the top side of the fillet and place in the pan spice side down. Cook for about 4 minutes per side, until cooked through.

3 Cut the French bread into 6 portions and slice them lengthwise to open into a sandwich. If you'd like, you can toast the bread under a broiler for a moment, but it is not necessary.

4 Spread the Roasted Tomato Tartar Sauce on both sides of the bread slices. Lay 1 piece of catfish on the bread, followed by 2 slices of tomato and some shredded lettuce.

2 tablespoons canola oil

6 (5-to 7-ounce) catfish fillets

2 tablespoons Blackening Spice (page 29)

2 loaves French bread

Roasted Tomato Tartar Sauce (page 38)

12 slices ripe tomato

Shredded iceberg lettuce

SERVES 6

GRILLED
LOBSTER

3 (1½-pound) lobsters

MAKES about 4 cups of diced lobster meat

Grilling gives a subtle, smoky flavor to lobster—something you miss when you boil it—so give this method a shot. Just like with crabs, there will always be someone who will run at the thought of killing and cooking a lobster, so give fair warning if you have guests who might be undone by witnessing the event.

1 The first step is to kill the lobster. With its claws bound by rubber bands, place the lobster on a cutting board, facing you. Place the point of a large, sharp chef's knife at the top of the head and push the blade down between the eyes. This kills the lobster instantly, even though the muscles continue to move.

2 Remove the tail by holding the body in one hand and the tail in the other and twisting in the opposite direction.

3 Flatten each tail and place a skewer through each, down the length of the tail and underside of the shell—this keeps them straight while grilling. Crack the claws with the backside of the knife.

4 Preheat your grill to high heat, and when hot, add presoaked wood chunks or chips. Grill the lobster, covered: The tails will take 8 to 10 minutes and the claws 12 to 14 minutes. You can tell it is done when the shell turns bright red. You don't want to overcook the lobster because it can turn anywhere from rubbery to mushy if overcooked.

5 Let the lobster cool a little before pulling it out of its shell and eating it or cutting it up for a lobster roll.

GRILLED LOBSTER ROLL

For a great variation on the traditional New England summery treat, we grill lobster, toss with some simple ingredients, and pile it on top of a warmed, butter-toasted bun. It'll give any restaurant in Maine a run for its money.

1 recipe Grilled Lobster, diced (page 188)

1 cup minced celery

¼ cup minced red onion

½ cup mayonnaise

2 teaspoons fresh lemon juice

½ teaspoon celery seed

¼ teaspoon salt

¼ teaspoon ground black pepper

8 potato hot-dog buns

2 tablespoons unsalted butter, softened

SERVES 8

1 In a large bowl, combine the lobster meat with the celery, onion, mayonnaise, lemon juice, celery seed, salt, and pepper, mixing well.

2 Spread the inside of each roll with the butter and set on a griddle pan, cast-iron pan, or sauté pan. You can also use the grill, but be careful, because the bread will burn easily. We prefer the taste you get from a pan. Toast the buttered side until golden. Fill with the lobster and serve.

WILD STRIPED BASS

WITH SMOKED TOMATO MOJO

This *mojo*, although nontraditional, lends a great taste to striped bass as well as other fish, meat, and poultry dishes.

1 **Make the smoked tomato *mojo*:** Core the tomatoes and cut them in half. Place them in a pan (that will go into a smoker or on the grill) and season with salt and pepper. Prepare your smoker or grill for barbecuing, using the indirect heat setup (see page 15), and preheat to 200°F. Have wood chunks or chips soaking and ready to go. When you're ready to cook, add the presoaked wood and oil the hot grate. Smoke the tomatoes, with the grill or smoker cover closed, for 45 minutes to an hour.

2 Let the tomatoes cool, then peel off the skin (it should come right off). Place 3 halves in a blender with the garlic, oregano, oil, 1 teaspoon of salt, and ½ teaspoon of pepper and blend until smooth. Cut the remaining tomato half into a small dice and add it to the mixture, along with the onion, without blending.

3 Preheat your grill to high and have wood chunks or chips soaking and ready to go. Make sure the grill grates are very clean and well oiled. Brush the fish with oil and season with salt and pepper.

4 Place the fish skin side down and grill for about 4 minutes, then turn and grill for about 4 minutes more. This could vary depending on the thickness of the fish.

5 Serve with the *mojo* on top or on the side.

FOR THE SMOKED TOMATO *MOJO:*

2 large ripe but firm beefsteak tomatoes

1 teaspoon kosher salt, plus more for seasoning the tomatoes

½ teaspoon ground black pepper, plus more for seasoning the tomatoes

1 garlic clove

¼ cup fresh oregano leaves

¼ cup olive oil

2 teaspoons finely diced red onion

2½ to 3 pounds wild striped bass, with skin, cut into 6 portions

Olive oil

Salt and ground black pepper

SERVES 6

PLANK-GRILLED
MAHI MAHI

FOR THE MARINADE:

6 scallions, cut into
2-inch pieces

3 tablespoons Dijon mustard

1 tablespoon honey

2 teaspoons fresh thyme

1 teaspoon salt

½ teaspoon ground
black pepper

3 tablespoons olive oil

★

2 to 2½ pounds mahi mahi
fillets

2 grilling planks, soaked
for 2 hours

SERVES 6

We used a plank here because it's a great method of cooking and adds a nice wood flavor to the fish. The edges of the plank burn just a bit, so some of the smoke infuses the fish. Keep a water bottle handy, because when you open up the cover, the plank will flame up. Just be sure you're not hitting the fish with the water.

1 Combine the ingredients for the marinade in a blender and blend until smooth.

2 Place the mahi mahi in a large bowl or in a zip-top bag, coat the fish with the marinade, cover the bowl or seal the bag, and marinate in the refrigerator for up to 1 hour.

3 Preheat your grill to high.

4 Place the mahi mahi on the planks and then onto the grill. Keep the lid closed while cooking—otherwise, the plank will flare up. Cook through for 15 to 20 minutes.

PLANK GRILLING: I THOUGHT YOU MIGHT LIKE A LITTLE TIDBIT OF knowledge surrounding this method of cookin'. The concept of plank grilling began centuries ago with the Native Americans. This process of cooking fish, split down the middle and secured to a plank of wood, is very effective in that it cooks in its own juices, keeping the meat moist, flavorful, and healthy. Native Americans typically used cedar because of the legendary healing powers it possessed, but now you can get planks in any variety of wood. Like wood smoking, plank grilling on different boards helps lend a great flavor to the fish. The types that we like the best include apple, cherry, cedar, and alder. Don't use just any wood—make sure it's specifically made for grilling. If you take wood from the lumberyard, you'll end up ingesting a heavy dose of formaldehyde—which never tastes good. Also, make sure you've soaked your planks in water for a substantial amount of time, so you don't open up the grill to find a plank engulfed in flames. You want the fish to be cooked, but not burned to a crisp.

SHRIMP 'N GRITS

A classic Southern dish; the scallions give a nice flavor and crunch to the creamy grits.

1 To make the grits, pour 4 cups of water into a 2-quart saucepan and add the salt. Place over medium-high heat and bring to a boil. Add the grits, whisking rapidly. Turn the heat down and simmer for about 5 minutes, whisking occasionally. If the grits seem too thick, add a little hot water to thin them out.

2 Melt the butter in a large sauté pan over medium heat. Add the onions and garlic and sauté until the onion is softened but not brown, about 5 minutes. Add the shrimp and Old Bay and sauté until the shrimp are just cooked, 4 to 5 minutes (they should be pink with no traces of gray). Add the scallions and squeeze in the juice from the lemons. Toss to incorporate and remove from the heat.

3 Divide the grits among 6 plates and place the shrimp in the center of the grits.

2 teaspoons salt

1 cup white grits

6 tablespoons unsalted butter

1 large Spanish onion, diced small

1½ tablespoons chopped garlic

2 pounds medium to large shrimp, peeled and deveined

2½ teaspoons Old Bay seasoning

4 scallions, green parts only, thinly sliced

2 to 3 lemons, halved

SERVES 6

SOFT-SHELL CRABS

WITH ANCHO CHILE-LIME BUTTER & AVOCADO

FOR THE ANCHO CHILE-LIME BUTTER:

½ cup (1 stick) unsalted butter, softened

1½ teaspoons lime zest

½ teaspoon fresh lime juice

¾ teaspoon ancho chile powder

¼ teaspoon salt

2 to 4 tablespoons olive oil

1 cup all-purpose flour

12 medium to large soft-shell crabs, cleaned (see Note)

3 avocados

SERVES 6

The flavored butter makes this dish smell (and taste) amazing. You'll want to keep extra nearby for dipping the meat in. Your crabs should be alive when you buy them, so make sure there aren't any squeamish guests around when it comes time for the clawed critters to meet the pan. (The season for soft-shell crab is from early May to mid-September, with a peak in June and July, so those are the best months to make this dish.)

1 **Make the ancho chile–lime butter:** Combine all the ingredients in a medium bowl and mix well.

2 Heat 2 tablespoons of the oil in a large sauté pan over medium-high heat. Place the flour in a shallow bowl, dredge the crabs in the flour, and place in the pan, working in batches. Cook for 4 minutes per side; add the remaining oil if the pan seems dry.

3 To serve, slice the avocados and place one half on each plate with 2 crabs and a dollop of the butter.

> **NOTE** You will need to clean the crabs, or you can ask your fishmonger to do it for you. Once cleaned, soft-shell crabs should be prepared that day or the next at the latest. If you purchase whole live crabs, store them on ice in the refrigerator in an uncovered container.
>
> To clean soft-shell crabs, use a pair of poultry shears to quickly cut off the front of the crab about ¼ inch behind the eyes and mouth. This kills the crab. Reach under the pointed edge of each side of the top shell to reveal the gills. Pull them out and discard them. Turn the crab over and pull off the bottom part of the shell, called the apron. Rinse the entire crab well and pat dry.

BBQ OYSTERS

WITH GRILLED JALAPEÑO MIGNONETTE

We like a nice meaty Blue Point oyster from the northeast, but you can use your favorite variety—the more local, the better. The jalapeño mignonette is also great on fresh-shucked raw oysters.

1 Scrub the oysters and keep them on ice until ready to use.

2 **Make the grilled jalapeño mignonette:** Preheat your grill to high and have wood chips soaking and ready to go. (We recommend a mild wood, such as apple or cherry, for oysters.) When the grill is hot, add the wood. Grill the jalapeño until it starts to wrinkle and char. Remove it and set aside to cool.

3 Peel the skin off the jalapeño, open it up, and remove the stem and seeds. Finely mince the jalapeño, place in a bowl, and add the shallot, vinegar, oil, and salt.

4 Place the oysters on the grill, cover, and cook for 8 to 10 minutes, until they start to open. Remove them from the grill, trying to retain as much of their liquid as possible.

5 Let them cool for a minute and pry them all the way open with an oyster knife, bottle opener, or screwdriver. Discard the top shell, which is the flatter side.

6 Sever the muscle that connects the meat to the shells and put a little mignonette on top of each.

3 dozen large oysters

FOR THE GRILLED JALAPEÑO MIGNONETTE:

1 jalapeño

1 tablespoon finely minced shallot

¼ cup champagne vinegar

1 tablespoon fruity extra-virgin olive oil

½ teaspoon salt, or to taste

SERVES 6

GRILLED TUNA

WITH SUMMER CORN RELISH

FOR THE CORN RELISH:

1½ teaspoons mustard seeds

2 tablespoons olive oil

1 cup diced Spanish onion

4 ears corn, kernels cut from the cobs

½ teaspoon sugar

2 tablespoons cider vinegar

1 teaspoon salt

½ teaspoon ground black pepper

1 red pepper, diced

1 green pepper, diced

3 pounds thick-cut tuna steak

Oil

Salt and ground black pepper

SERVES 6

Be forewarned: The mustard seeds will start to pop out of the pan if they get too hot. Although this is pretty comical, the flying seeds are hot and not easy to dodge (so don't stick your face near the pan), but the tiny projectiles are worth it for this delicious summer meal.

1 In a large sauté pan over low heat, toast the mustard seeds. When you can see the seeds starting to pop, add the oil, followed by the onion, and raise the heat to medium. Cook for 2 minutes, then add the corn and sugar.

2 Cook, stirring, for 2 to 3 minutes more, until the corn is cooked through. Transfer to a bowl to cool for 10 minutes.

3 Add the remaining relish ingredients to the bowl and set aside.

4 Preheat your grill to high and have wood chips soaked and ready to go on.

5 Just before you before you're ready to cook, place the presoaked wood on the hot coals and oil the hot grates. Lightly oil the tuna, season with salt and pepper, and place on the grill. Turn the pieces of tuna 45 degrees before flipping over to give them nice grill marks. It will take 3 to 4 minutes per side for rare and 5 to 6 minutes for medium.

6 Slice the tuna and serve with the corn relish.

GRILLED
SALMON
WITH GUAVA BBQ SAUCE

FOR THE RUB:

¾ teaspoon smoked paprika

2¼ teaspoons chili powder

¾ teaspoon ground cumin

¾ teaspoon ground coriander

¾ teaspoon ground
black pepper

¾ teaspoon kosher salt

¾ teaspoon granulated sugar

★

Canola oil

6 salmon fillets (about 3 pounds
total)

1 recipe Guava BBQ Sauce
(page 32)

SERVES 6

This is a nice twist on the traditional grilled salmon fillet; it gives your taste buds a contrast of flavors to enjoy—a smoky, savory rub paired with a lightly sweet and tropical basting sauce. This dish pairs well with Spiced String Beans (page 222) and Grits (page 210).

1 Preheat your grill to medium-high heat.

2 Combine the rub ingredients in a small bowl.

3 Lightly oil the salmon and dust both sides with the rub.

4 Just before you're ready to cook, oil the hot grate. Grill the salmon, with the cover on, for 3 to 4 minutes per side, brushing the salmon with the Guava BBQ Sauce before you turn it. Brush the top again before serving. Serve with extra sauce.

SWEET & SPICY
CATFISH

We created this when our St. Maarten franchise opened in the Caribbean. It's a great dish, and the flavors from the sweetened butter and the rub meld together nicely on the fish.

1 recipe Spicy Fish Rub (page 26)

¾ cup (1½ sticks) unsalted butter, softened

6 tablespoons brown sugar

⅛ teaspoon salt

2 to 3 tablespoons olive oil

6 skinless catfish fillets (about 3 pounds total)

SERVES 6

1 In a small bowl, combine 5½ teaspoons of the Spicy Fish Rub with the butter, brown sugar, and salt. Mix well and set aside at room temperature.

2 Heat the oil in a large sauté pan over medium heat. Pat the catfish fillets dry and dust both sides of the fish with the remaining Spicy Fish Rub. Place the catfish in the pan and reduce the heat to medium-low. Cook on each side for 5 to 6 minutes.

3 Remove from the pan to a platter or individual plates and top with a dollop of the butter.

DRINKS: HELP WASH DOWN YOUR SEAFOOD with these cocktails:

HURRICANE

A classic New Orleans concoction that goes well with any seafood dish. And you get to use those nifty Hurricane glasses. See the recipe on page 60.

LOUISVILLE LEMONADE

The Kentucky version of the Lynchburg Lemonade, the taste of Maker's Mark in the glass lets you know it's working. See the recipe on page 53.

PALMETTO PUNCH

Because this festive bowl-based beverage is made with spiced rum and a Myers's floater, it's the perfect choice for those looking for something sweet with a little kick. See the recipe on page 54.

SCALLOPS

GRILLED WITH LEMON ZEST & THYME

3 pounds sea scallops

FOR THE MARINADE:

Zest of 4 lemons

1 tablespoon chopped fresh thyme

½ to 1 teaspoon salt

½ teaspoon ground black pepper

3 tablespoons olive oil

SERVES 6 to 8

When you have fresh sea scallops, you don't need to do much to make them tasty—a little seasoning goes a long way.

1 Pull the muscle off the scallops.

2 Combine the ingredients for the marinade in a large bowl and gently toss in the scallops. Cover and refrigerate until ready to grill, no more than 2 hours.

3 Preheat your grill to high heat and have wood chunks or chips soaking and ready to go.

4 Just before you're ready to cook, add the wood and oil the hot grate. Grill the scallops, covered, for 1 to 2 minutes per side. If you overcook scallops, they can become rubbery.

SHRIMP BOIL
WITH POTATOES & CORN

1 package crawfish/crab boil seasoning (available at most fish markets)

1 large Spanish onion, halved

3 lemons, halved

1½ pounds small new potatoes

6 ears corn, cut into thirds

4 pounds medium shrimp, unpeeled

SERVES 8

The traditional and quintessential Southern standard. Just make sure you have plenty of shrimp to go around for your party; novice boilers always make too few.

1 In a large stockpot, combine 8 quarts of water with the boil seasoning, onion, and lemons. Place over high heat and bring to a boil.

2 Boil for 8 to 10 minutes, then add the potatoes and boil for 5 minutes more.

3 Add the corn and shrimp, bring back to a boil, and turn off the heat. Let it sit for 2 minutes more, drain, and serve.

HOW TO EAT A CRAWFISH: THERE IS A LEVEL OF EFFICIENCY at eating
that makes you enjoy it more. This is why first-time crawfish-boilers often stare in amazement while everyone around them puts down three mudbugs in the time it takes them to get through with one. But when you're good at it, there's no work at all.

STEP ONE
The trick to eating crawfish is to grab the tail and the body and twist it, then give the head a quick suck and inhale. I find this particularly hard, given my lack of thumbs, but it does give you a mist of spicy flavor.

STEP TWO
Depending on how much meat is exposed on the remaining tail, you'll have to determine if you want to go after that. The quicker you eat, the more you eat. If there's enough meat exposed and overflowing from the shell, get your teeth in there and grab the firm meat with your front teeth while pinching the bottom of the tail, releasing the bottom of the meat from the shell, and you can pull the whole thing out.

STEP THREE
If you can't get your teeth onto firm meat, you'll peel back the back shell—one layer only—and expose some of the firm meat and repeat the pinching and pulling from step two.

A final tip: The ground will be littered with carcasses, so hopefully there's a garbage pail nearby or else four-legged friends such as myself will have a field day with your lawn.

WHAT TO PUT IN A BOIL: CRAWFISH, SHRIMP, AND CRAB—each used for the
boil—often come from Louisiana's own backyard waters: the Gulf of Mexico and Lake Pontchartrain. Caught by net, using a piece of meat to attract the submerged crustaceans, it's not long after that they're dumped directly into the pot, which can sometimes be filled with seawater because the salt helps to flavor the boil. The setup is rudimentary. The pots can go up to 30 gallons, but folks typically use the largest one they can find. Perched atop an outside burner and fit with a colander to hold the seafood, into the water go lemons and a heap of spices—a mixture premade by the boil kings, Zatarain's. Once the aromatic concoction comes to a rolling boil, in go the corn on the cob, potatoes, and other root vegetables. Last comes the main attraction: the seafood.

Here you've got some choices for your shellfish. If you're using crawfish in your boil, which is the regional choice for Louisiana, then you're one step closer to the traditional boil. Just make sure you clean them per your fishmonger's recommendations. Boil 'em for about twenty minutes, then let them soak in the liquid for another ten. It's that extra time that allows all that flavor to get soaked up by the mudbugs—as they're colloquially dubbed down South—and make them particularly satisfying. When you crack into a crawfish, the true boil champions will twist the head off and suck the juices out of it, which are spicy, briny, and delicious. This often freaks out the uninitiated and any squeamish ladies present, but the hidden pocket of flavor is always spot on.

If you're going with crab, don't forget the mallets. It'll be a little hard to get the meat out of the hard shells otherwise. If you can get hold of Maryland blue claws, pulled directly from the Chesapeake Bay, we recommend them. When they come out of the boil, remember to generously sprinkle Old Bay Seasoning on them. It makes them extra delicious. Or you could keep some ancho chile–lime butter spread on hand, from our amazing soft-shell crab recipe, to dip the meat in. The crabs' claws occasionally do hurt, especially when you're transferring them to the pot, so wear gloves or have some long tongs nearby, although real troopers just show the red marks of pinching with pride at the table later.

When you try this at home, whatever's going into the pot is up to you. The only real tip we'll give you is to be careful with the amount of spice in the mixture, because the corn and potatoes tend to absorb the heat quickly and can get taste-bud-searing hot if you're not careful. But as to what spices are in the mix, that's also your call. The only thing that should remain consistent is the fun atmosphere swirling around the vat of gurgling seafood. And the fact that you have to spread out newspaper on a lengthy table upon which the shellfish gets poured when it's done in the boil just makes the whole affair more authentic.

PAN-FRIED REDFISH
WITH GREEN TOMATO RELISH

Redfish, also called red drum, is a common Southern fish, similar to snapper. White and mild, redfish soaks up all the other flavors well, giving the dish a nice spice. If you can't find redfish, you can substitute snapper or striped bass.

1 **Prepare the relish:** Combine all the relish ingredients in a medium nonreactive saucepan, cover, and place over low heat.

2 Bring to a simmer and cook for about 30 minutes, until the vegetables are soft. You should notice an increase in liquid in the pot, which is good. Remove from the heat and set aside to cool.

3 Season the fish on both sides with salt and pepper.

4 Heat a cast-iron or nonstick sauté pan until just about smoking; add 1 or 2 tablespoons of oil. Put the fish in the pan and cook until cooked through and golden, about 3 minutes per side, depending on the thickness of the fish.

5 Place the fish on individual plates or a platter and spoon the relish on top.

FOR THE RELISH:

2 cups diced green tomato

½ cup diced green pepper

½ cup diced Spanish onion

½ teaspoon mustard seeds

1½ teaspoons salt

1½ teaspoons sugar

¼ cup champagne vinegar

½ teaspoon ground black pepper

3 pounds redfish fillets, cut into 6 portions

Salt and ground black pepper

Olive oil

SERVES 6

CHAPTER 10

SIDES

SIDE DISHES HAVE PROVEN

THEIR VAST VERSATILITY TIME AND AGAIN. THEY

can spruce up any meal or double as a feast on their own. Their place in the heart of Southern cooking is no different. There'd be no festivities without a well-stocked array of sides adorning the table, situated in between the steaming plates of meat and main dishes.

The sides really do make the meal, and they're often what you find yourself snacking on late into the evening, after your party or event is over. When it's 3 A.M., and you're a little tipsy and you start yanking containers out of the refrigerator, side dishes allow you to grab one spoonful of yumminess with such ease. Possibly because of their popularity in college dorms (mac and cheese), holiday meals (candied yams on Thanksgiving), or just the ease of cooking (BBQ baked beans), side dishes—or trimmings, as they are sometimes called—represent the absolute essence of comfort food. And at Brother Jimmy's, we do the most comfortable food of all.

Which is why Southern sides, from the staples of mac and cheese and grits to baked beans and collard greens, are tried and true plates that help bolster the wow factor in any barbecue and can stand as whole meals in their own right (we think you can name one friend who chows down on *only* the sides every time you eat). In fact, in our restaurants, we even serve four of our sides together as a main course.

Many sides also have a deep history in the Southern way of life, too. For example, black-eyed peas and collards are traditionally eaten on New Year's Day down South. The way the ideology goes, families must cook, serve, and eat some black-eyed peas and collard greens on the first day of any new year to ensure good luck and prosperity. Most often it's said that the black-eyed peas bring good fortune, while the greens represent more money. Please let us know if that works when you try it.

And sides double as fixins, which make any sandwich better. That's why pulled pork sandwich aficionados liberally heap coleslaw between the buns. Or why a large dollop of mashed potatoes and gravy on a turkey sandwich never fails to delight eager stomachs.

However you want to serve it—as a side, on its own, or mixed together with a bit of everything else (remember "garbage plates" in college?)—our comprehensive list of savory dishes will please any palate. Even the veggies. Among our personal favorites? The Warm Potato Salad, because it is made with double-smoked bacon, and there's nothing the addition of bacon can't make extremely awesome. It's more addictive than chocolate, and it's highly likely that the bowl will be cleaned before you get to stow some away for later. Or you can whip up our grits in one of three ways—plain, cheese, and black pepper–scallion—so no matter how you like the Southern side dish mainstay, your stomach will be pleased.

CORNBREAD

1 cup cornmeal

1 cup all-purpose flour

½ cup sugar

½ teaspoon baking soda

½ teaspoon salt

2 large eggs

1 cup buttermilk

½ cup (1 stick) unsalted butter, melted and cooled

½ cup cooked corn kernels

SERVES 6 to 8

What's a Southern meal without cornbread? This staple is also great toasted with a little butter for breakfast or cut up to use for stuffing.

1 Preheat the oven to 350°F and grease a 9-by-9-inch square pan or an 8-inch cast-iron pan.

2 In a large bowl, combine the cornmeal, flour, sugar, baking soda, and salt.

3 In another large bowl, beat the eggs with the buttermilk and butter. Add the corn and then add the wet mixture to the dry mixture and mix just until incorporated.

4 Pour the batter into the prepared pan and bake for about 30 minutes, until a tester comes out clean.

5 Remove from the oven and let sit for 5 minutes before cutting.

GRILLED

SWEET PLANTAINS

These may not be considered traditional Southern food, but they are great with Puerto Rican *Mojo* Ribs (page 117) and Sweet and Spicy Catfish (page 199).

3 ripe plantains (they will be yellow and black)

3 tablespoons vegetable oil

Salt and ground black pepper

SERVES 6

1 With a sharp knife, make 3 or 4 score marks in the peel from top to bottom (this makes them easier to peel); try not to cut into the meat of the plantain. Peel the plantains.

2 Preheat your grill to medium heat.

3 Cut the plantains in half lengthwise, place in a large bowl, toss with the oil, and season with a little salt and pepper.

4 Grill the plantains for about 10 minutes, turning often, until they have some color and grill marks.

GRITS
(PLAIN, CHEESY & BLACK PEPPER-SCALLION)

PLAIN GRITS

1 teaspoon kosher salt,
or to taste

1 cup quick white grits

2 tablespoons unsalted butter

We've got your grits three ways, so no matter how you like 'em, you'll be happy.

1. To make plain grits, pour the water into a large saucepan and add the salt. Place over medium-high heat and bring to a boil.

2. While whisking, slowly pour the grits into the boiling water. Reduce the heat and continue whisking for about 5 minutes, until the grits have thickened.

3. Add the butter, taste, and add more salt if needed.

CHEESY GRITS

Add 1½ to 2 cups of grated sharp cheddar cheese to the cooked grits when you add the butter in Step 3, above. Stir continuously until the cheese is completely melted.

BLACK PEPPER-SCALLION GRITS

Add 4 thinly sliced scallions and ½ teaspoon ground black pepper to plain cooked grits when you add the butter in Step 3, above.

SWEET POTATO WEDGES

Not only healthier than french fries, sweet potato wedges have a sugary taste that can't be beat as an accompaniment to any protein.

. . . .

1 Preheat the oven to 350°F and line a baking sheet with parchment.

2 Cut the sweet potatoes into long wedges, ½ inch wide. Place in a bowl and toss with the oil, then toss with the cumin, coriander, cinnamon, chili powder, salt, and pepper.

3 Place the wedges on the baking sheet and bake for 20 to 30 minutes, until fork tender.

3 sweet potatoes

3 tablespoons olive oil

1 teaspoon ground cumin

1 teaspoon ground coriander

½ teaspoon ground cinnamon

2 teaspoons chili powder

1 teaspoon salt

¼ teaspoon ground black pepper

MAKES 6 to 8 servings

POTATO SALAD

This iconic side works well for picnics, warm summer days (though you should keep it as cold as you can), and any barbecue event.

. . . .

1 Place the potatoes in a large saucepan of water, place over medium-high heat, and bring to a boil. Reduce the heat and simmer until the potatoes until tender, about 15 minutes. Drain and set aside to cool.

2 Place the eggs in a small saucepan and cover with water by 2 inches. Bring just to a boil, then remove from the heat, cover, and let sit for 12 minutes. Remove the eggs from the hot water. Run under cold water until completely cooled, then peel, dice, and set aside.

3 In a large bowl, combine the remaining ingredients. Add the potatoes and eggs and mix well.

2 pounds Red Bliss potatoes, cut into 1-inch pieces, unpeeled

2 large eggs

½ cup Hellman's mayonnaise

¼ cup roughly chopped fresh cilantro

1 tablespoon white vinegar

2 tablespoons pickle relish

1 tablespoon spicy brown mustard, such as Gulden's

¼ cup diced Spanish onion

¼ cup diced red pepper

¼ cup diced green pepper

¼ cup small diced celery

1½ teaspoons salt

1 teaspoon ground black pepper

SERVES 6 to 8

SMOKY CORN & BLACK BEAN

CHOW CHOW

2 large beefsteak tomatoes

¼ teaspoon salt, plus more for seasoning the tomatoes

¼ teaspoon ground black pepper, plus more for seasoning the tomatoes

2 tablespoons olive oil

3 cups fresh corn kernels

1 (15-ounce) can black beans, drained and rinsed

¼ cup very thinly sliced red onion

¼ cup packed finely chopped cilantro

SERVES 6 to 8

In addition to being fun to say, this dish is delicious. It pairs well with a number of plates but can also be enjoyed on its own for lunch or a snack.

1 Core the tomatoes and cut them in half. Place cut side up in a heatproof pan and sprinkle with a little bit of salt and pepper. Prepare your smoker or grill for barbecuing, using the indirect heat setup (see page 15), and preheat to 200°F. Add presoaked wood chips or chunks and place the pan with the tomatoes in the grill or smoker and smoke, covered, for about 45 minutes. Remove the tomatoes and cool.

2 Pull the skin off the tomatoes and chop them.

3 Heat the oil in a medium sauté pan over medium heat. Add the corn kernels and ¼ teaspoon of salt and sauté until just cooked, 3 to 4 minutes. Remove from the heat, transfer to a bowl, and cool.

4 Add the chopped tomatoes and remaining ingredients to the bowl with the corn and mix well. Adjust the seasoning if necessary.

PERFECT
GRILLED VEGGIES

For this grilled veggie platter, we typically use squash, zucchini, peppers, portobellos, sweet onions, asparagus, and eggplant, but there's no reason you can't mix and match as your meal and tastes dictate. Other solid options include corn, string beans, and potatoes. These herb-and-lemon marinated veggies are also great in a sandwich.

1 In a medium bowl, combine all the ingredients for the marinade.

2 Slice the squash, zucchini, and eggplant into about ¼-inch-thick rounds. Trim the hard, woody ends of the asparagus by holding the very bottom of the stems and gently pushing with your fingers about midway up to the right or left until it snaps. Remove the stem from the mushrooms and cut the pepper lengthwise into 4 pieces. Remove the stem and any remaining core or seeds. Cut the onions into rounds a little thicker than ¼ inch.

3 Place the squash, zucchini, asparagus, and pepper in a large bowl and pour the marinade over top; toss gently to coat. (Tossing would cause the onion slices to break apart into rings and the fragile mushrooms to break.) Using a slotted spoon, transfer the marinade-tossed vegetables to a tray. Brush the onion rounds and mushrooms on both sides with the remaining marinade, and place on the tray with the other vegetables. Pour any remaining marinade over top of the vegetables and set them aside to marinate for about 15 minutes.

4 Preheat your grill to moderate heat; you can use a little presoaked wood if you want, as long as it is a mild one, such as cherry or apple.

5 Just before you're ready to cook, oil the hot grate. Grill the vegetables for a couple of minutes on each side. The asparagus can be rolled back and forth until it looks done. All the vegetables should maintain their bright colors.

6 Serve hot or cold.

FOR THE MARINADE:

½ cup chopped fresh oregano

½ cup chopped fresh flat-leaf Italian parsley leaves

2 tablespoons chopped fresh thyme

4 garlic cloves, minced or finely grated

Zest of 3 lemons

Juice of 2 lemons

4 teaspoons salt

1½ teaspoons ground black pepper

½ cup olive oil

1 yellow squash

1 zucchini

1 Italian eggplant or 2 Japanese eggplants

1 bunch asparagus

3 portobello mushrooms

1 red pepper

1 large or 2 small sweet onion(s)

SERVES 6

WARM

POTATO SALAD

2 pounds new potatoes, cut into quarters or eighths depending on the size

1½ teaspoons salt, or to taste

4 slices applewood-smoked bacon

1 cup finely diced Spanish onion

2 tablespoons chopped fresh thyme

2 tablespoons champagne vinegar

¼ teaspoon ground black pepper

SERVES 6

After eating this warm treat, nearly every other potato salad will taste like it was made in a shoe. The applewood-smoked bacon gives it a nice meaty flavor, and the onion lends a bit of crunch to each bite.

1 Place the potatoes in a pot of water with 1 teaspoon of the salt and bring to a boil. Reduce the heat and simmer for 8 to 10 minutes, until the potatoes are tender and can be pierced with a fork. Drain the potatoes and place them in a large bowl.

2 Cut the bacon crosswise into thin slices and place in a sauté pan over low heat to render out the fat and crisp it up a bit.

3 When the bacon is starting to get crisp, add the onions and cook until softened, about 5 minutes.

4 Remove from the heat and add the thyme, vinegar, remaining salt, and pepper. Add to the potatoes, mixing well to distribute the dressing.

5 Serve warm.

SWEET

POTATO SALAD

Because sometimes your potato salad should be a bit sweet.

1 Preheat the oven to 350°F and line a baking sheet with parchment.

2 In a large bowl, toss the sweet potatoes with 2 tablespoons of the oil, 1 teaspoon of the salt, and ¼ teaspoon of the pepper. Place on the lined baking sheet, place in the oven, and roast for about 35 minutes, until tender but not mushy. Remove from the oven and set aside to cool.

3 Cut the corn off the cob. Heat 2 tablespoons of the remaining oil in a medium sauté pan over medium heat. Add the corn kernels and sauté for 5 to 6 minutes, until tender but not mushy. Remove from the heat and set aside to cool.

4 Combine the sweet potatoes and corn in a large bowl. Add the scallions, red peppers, lemon juice, coriander, paprika, the remaining oil, the remaining salt, and the remaining black pepper, gently mixing to incorporate all the ingredients.

3 medium sweet potatoes, cut into ¾-inch chunks (about 6 cups)

7½ tablespoons olive oil

1½ teaspoons salt

½ teaspoon ground black pepper

2 ears corn

2 scallions, thinly sliced

½ cup minced red pepper

1½ tablespoons fresh lemon juice

¾ teaspoon ground coriander

½ teaspoon smoked paprika

SERVES 6

BBQ
BAKED
BEANS
WITH SMOKED PORK

1 tablespoon olive oil

¾ cup diced Spanish onion

32 ounces pork and beans
(two 16-ounce cans or one
32-ounce can)

4 ounces smoked pork butt,
cut into 1- or 2-inch cubes
(about 1 cup)

½ cup Brother Jimmy's Original
BBQ Sauce (page 31)

1 tablespoon molasses (we like
Grandma's Molasses)

SERVES 6 to 8

The smoked pork adds a nice flavor to this Southern classic, but you should feel free to add a little diced bacon to maximize your pork ingestion.

1 Prepare your smoker or grill for barbecuing, using the indirect heat setup (see page 15), and preheat to 240°F. Have wood chunks or chips soaking and ready to go.

2 In a small frying pan, heat the oil over medium heat. Add the onions and sauté until soft and translucent, about 5 minutes. Remove from the heat and set aside.

3 In a large bowl, mix together the pork and beans, smoked pork butt, sautéed onion, BBQ Sauce, and molasses and place in a shallow baking dish.

4 Add the presoaked wood and baking dish with beans to your grill or smoker and smoke, covered, for 45 minutes.

CANDIED YAMS WITH WALNUTS

It doesn't have to be Thanksgiving to enjoy candied yams. This is simple enough to do more than once a year and tastes fantastic. These also pair astoundingly well with Fried Chicken or Grilled Chipotle-Orange Pork Loin (pages 158 or 123).

4 yams, cut into 1½-inch chunks

1 lemon, sliced into very thin rounds

½ cup walnuts, lightly crushed

1½ cups brown sugar

1 cup corn syrup

1¼ cups maple syrup

3½ teaspoons ground cinnamon

1 teaspoon ground nutmeg

1¾ cups orange juice

6 tablespoons (¾ stick) unsalted butter

½ teaspoon kosher salt

SERVES 6 to 8

1 Preheat the oven to 350°F.

2 Combine the yams, lemon slices, and walnuts into a 3-quart baking dish.

3 Combine the remaining ingredients in a large saucepan, place over medium heat, and cook until the sugar is dissolved, about 10 minutes.

4 Pour the hot syrup over the yams and cover the dish with aluminum foil.

5 Bake for 30 to 40 minutes, until the yams are beginning to get tender. Remove the foil and bake, uncovered, for 15 minutes more.

WILD RICE SALAD

A perfect accompaniment to any dish, you can also add grilled chicken to the mix and turn this into a meal on its own.

1 Place the wild rice in a saucepan with 4 cups of water. Place over medium-high heat and bring to a boil. Cover, reduce the heat, and simmer for 40 to 60 minutes, until tender. Set aside to cool.

2 Roast the poblano by placing it over an open flame; a hot grill or a gas burner on your home stove works well. Turn it frequently until the skin chars and starts to blister from the flame. Place the chile in a small bowl and cover with plastic wrap, or seal it in an airtight container. Let rest for 10 to 15 minutes—this allows the skin to separate from the meat a little and makes for easier peeling. When the chile is cool enough to handle, peel off all the charred skin and remove the seeds. Cut into ½-inch squares.

3 Cut the corn kernels off the cob. Heat 1 tablespoon oil in a medium frying pan over medium heat. Add the corn kernels and ½ teaspoon salt and sauté until just tender, about 3 to 4 minutes. Remove from the heat and set aside to cool.

4 Combine the wild rice, poblano, and corn in a large bowl. Add the remaining oil, remaining salt, the onion, cilantro, and vinegar and toss well.

1 cup wild rice

1 poblano chile

2 ears corn

2 tablespoons olive oil

1 teaspoon kosher salt

¾ cup sweet very thinly sliced onion (such as Vidalia)

¼ cup finely chopped fresh cilantro

4 teaspoons red wine vinegar

SERVES 6

BLACK-EYED PEAS WITH BACON

1 pound dried black-eyed peas

12 ounces bacon (about
15 slices), diced

2½ cups diced Spanish onion

6 cups chicken stock
(store-bought is fine)

½ teaspoon cayenne pepper

1 tablespoon chopped
fresh thyme

¾ teaspoon rubbed sage leaves

1 teaspoon kosher salt,
plus more if needed

1 bay leaf

SERVES 6 to 8

This Southern staple gets better with the addition of bacon.

1 Sort through the peas and remove any dirt or small stones. Place in a container with double the amount of water and let soak overnight. (See Note for a quick soak method.)

2 Place the bacon in a large saucepan over low heat and cook to render the fat.

3 When the bacon starts to become crisp, about 5 to 6 minutes, add the diced onion and cook until translucent, about five additional minutes.

4 Drain the water from the peas, give them a quick rinse, and add to the pan with the bacon and onion.

5 Add the remaining ingredients to the pan, increase the heat to medium-high, and bring to a boil. Reduce the heat and simmer for 30 to 45 minutes, until tender. Taste and add more salt if needed.

NOTE If you don't have time to soak the peas overnight, use the quick-soak method: Place them in a pot and add water to cover. Bring to a rolling boil, then remove from the heat immediately. Let sit for 1 hour and proceed with the recipe.

MASHED POTATOES
WITH WHITE GRAVY

The epitome of comfort food, mashed potatoes and gravy go great with absolutely anything you're serving. To kick up the flavor a notch, we use our own mashed potato spice blend. If you're feeling particularly adventurous, add some chives, rosemary or horseradish.

1 Wash the potatoes—but don't peel them—and cut them into chunks. Place them in a large saucepan and add enough water to cover by 2 inches.

2 Bring to a boil, then reduce the heat to medium and simmer until the potatoes are very tender, 20 to 30 minutes.

3 In a small saucepan, combine the milk, cream, butter, salt, and spices.

4 Drain the potatoes, return them to the pot, and add half of the warm milk mixture.

5 Using a potato masher, break up the potatoes; slowly add the remaining milk mixture, until the potatoes have a creamy consistency (although they won't be perfectly smooth).

6 Serve with the White Gravy.

4 pounds Idaho (or Russet) potatoes

1¾ cups milk

½ cup heavy cream

6 tablespoons (¾ stick) unsalted butter

2½ teaspoons kosher salt

½ teaspoon rubbed sage leaves

½ teaspoon ground dried thyme

½ teaspoon ground black pepper

⅛ teaspoon ground white pepper

White Gravy (page 146)

SERVES 6 to 8

COLLARD GREENS

3 to 4 pounds collard greens

8 cups chicken stock
(store-bought is fine)

3 tablespoons olive oil

1½ teaspoons granulated garlic

2½ teaspoons kosher salt

½ teaspoon granulated onion

¼ teaspoon cayenne pepper

½ teaspoon crushed
red pepper flakes

½ teaspoon ground
black pepper

¼ teaspoon ground
white pepper

SERVES 6 to 8

Although this recipe is delicious as is, you can substitute other liquids—like beer, which gives a nice finish—for some of the chicken stock for an equally good effect.

1 Remove the stems from the collard greens by pushing your thumb and index finger against the thickest part of the stem going upward toward the top of the leaf. Wash and drain. Slice the leaves into wide strips.

2 Combine the remaining ingredients in a stockpot and bring to a boil.

3 Add the collard greens, reduce the heat, and simmer for 20 to 30 minutes, until they are tender but still have a bite to them. It will appear as if there isn't enough liquid to cook all the greens in, but as soon as they start cooking, they will shrink down a lot.

SPICED STRING BEANS

8 cups water

2 teaspoons granulated garlic

1¼ teaspoons paprika

1 teaspoon granulated onion

⅛ teaspoon cayenne pepper

⅛ teaspoon ground white pepper

2 teaspoons salt

2½ pounds string beans,
trimmed

3 tablespoons unsalted butter

SERVES 6 to 8

These spiced beans are a very popular side dish with a nice kick to them, thanks to the cayenne and white pepper.

1 Place the water in a large saucepan and bring to a boil over high heat.

2 In a small bowl, combine the spices and salt.

3 When the water comes to a boil, add the string beans. Wait for the water to come back to a boil and cook the string beans for 1 minute longer, or until tender but still with a bite. Drain.

4 Place the butter in the now empty pot over low heat and melt it. Return the string beans to the pot with the butter and add the spice mixture a little at a time until they are seasoned to your taste.

CORN
PUDDING

This Southern side dish is baked in a water bath, which helps give it a nice custardy texture. Served warm, there's nothing better than that first bite.

1 Preheat the oven to 400°F and butter a 1½-quart casserole dish.

2 Beat the eggs in a large bowl and set aside.

3 In a medium saucepan, melt 2 tablespoons butter over low heat. Whisk in the flour until smooth.

4 Slowly add the milk to the pan little by little, whisking constantly until it's all in and the mixture is smooth. Continue mixing until it thickens, about 5 minutes.

5 Slowly add about 1 cup of the hot milk mixture to the eggs and beat it to temper the eggs, then add the egg mixture back into the milk along with the sugar. With a wooden spoon or a rubber spatula, continue to stir the custard for a minute more. Remove from the heat.

6 Bring small saucepan of water to a boil.

7 Add the corn, scallions, salt, and pepper to the custard and pour into the casserole dish. Place the casserole into a roasting pan and pour enough boiling water into the pan to reach halfway up the sides.

8 Carefully place in the oven and bake for 25 to 35 minutes, until a small knife inserted in the center comes out clean.

2 tablespoons unsalted butter, softened, plus extra to grease the casserole

2 large eggs

3 tablespoons all-purpose flour

2 cups milk, warmed

½ teaspoon sugar

2½ cups fresh corn kernels

2 tablespoons thinly sliced scallion greens

½ teaspoon salt

¼ teaspoon ground black pepper

SERVES 6 to 8

BREAKOUT RECIPES

MAC & CHEESE

Remember when you were little and you'd play with your food, piling your mac and cheese high atop of your chicken, and then your mom or dad would yell at you to stop messing around and just eat it? And then you got to college, where all you did was devour mac and cheese straight from the microwave with whatever else you had handy tossed in—be that hot dogs, Cheetos, or chicken nuggets left over from the night before? Mac and cheese has been that constant dish that always delights and never disappoints, regardless of what you're mixing in there—even if it's a squirt of ketchup.

The dish has a history in the United States dating back to 1802, when our third president, Thomas Jefferson, first served the staple in the White House. Before coming to America, mac and cheese was an English concoction described as "macaroni baked with cream and cheese." Makes you wonder if they had it at the first Thanksgiving. And of course Kraft made it an American classic in the 1930s.

We've got five yummy recipes for you, the original and four variations. Whether you want it smoky, supremely cheesy, with a little bit of heat—courtesy of some smoky chili—or with a crunch (after it's been deep-fried), we've got you covered.

MAC & CHEESE

1 tablespoon kosher salt

1 pound elbow macaroni

6 tablespoons (¾ stick) unsalted butter

¾ cup diced Spanish onion

1 pound Velveeta, chopped

1 cup milk

½ teaspoon dry mustard

1½ cups panko (Japanese breadrumbs)

. . . .

1 Bring a pot of water to boil and add the salt. Add the macaroni and cook to al dente, 7 to 8 minutes.

2 Strain the pasta and rinse under cold water to stop the cooking. Set aside.

3 Melt 2 tablespoons of the butter in a small sauté pan over medium-low heat, add the onion, and cook until soft and translucent but without coloring.

4 Preheat the oven to 350°F.

5 In a double boiler, combine the Velveeta, milk, and mustard, stirring occasionally. When the cheese has all been incorporated and you have a smooth sauce, add the onions and mix well. Continue cooking until the sauce is thick enough that it doesn't run when you swipe a finger across the back of a wooden spoon that's been coated in it, about 10 minutes.

6 Combine the macaroni with the cheese sauce and pour into a casserole dish.

7 Melt the remaining 4 tablespoons of butter in the pan you cooked the onion in over medium heat. Add the panko and cook, stirring, for about 5 minutes, until golden brown. Remove from the heat and sprinkle the crumbs on top of the macaroni and cheese.

8 Place in the oven and bake for 30 to 40 minutes, until the top is golden and bubbly around the edges.

SERVES 6 to 8

SMOKED CHEDDAR MAC & CHEESE

1 tablespoon plus ½ teaspoon salt

1 pound elbow macaroni

6 tablespoons (¾ stick) unsalted butter

3 tablespoons all-purpose flour

2 cups milk

3½ cups grated smoked cheddar cheese

¼ teaspoon ground black pepper

1½ cups panko (Japanese breadcrumbs)

. . . .

1 Bring a pot of water to boil and add 1 tablespoon of the salt. Add the macaroni and cook to al dente, 7 to 8 minutes.

2 Strain the pasta and rinse under cold water to stop the cooking. Set aside.

3 Melt 2 tablespoons of the butter in a 2-quart saucepan over medium heat. Add the flour and cook, whisking constantly, for about 2 minutes until you have a roux.

4 Preheat the oven to 350°F.

5 In a small saucepan, warm the milk and, little by little, whisk it into the flour, breaking up any lumps as you go. Once all the milk has been added, cook for another minute or two until it starts to thicken. Be sure to scrape the sides.

6 Add 3 cups of the grated cheese, the remaining salt, and the pepper. Stir until the cheese is just incorporated. Add the macaroni and stir to coat. Pour into a baking dish and sprinkle the remaining ½ cup cheese on top.

7 Melt the remaining 4 tablespoons of butter in a medium frying pan over medium heat. Add the panko and cook, stirring, for about 5 minutes, until golden brown. Remove from the heat and sprinkle the crumbs on top of the macaroni and cheese.

8 Place in the oven and bake for 30 to 40 minutes, until the top is golden and bubbly around the edges.

SERVES 6 to 8

MAC & FOUR CHEESES

1 tablespoon plus ½ teaspoon salt

1 pound elbow macaroni

2 tablespoons unsalted butter

3 tablespoons all-purpose flour

2 cups milk

½ cup grated white cheddar cheese

½ cup grated Fontina cheese

½ cup grated Parrano Gouda cheese

½ cup grated cave-aged Gruyère cheese

¼ teaspoon ground black pepper

. . . .

1 Bring a pot of water to boil and add 1 tablespoon of the salt. Add the macaroni and cook to al dente, 7 to 8 minutes.

2 Strain the pasta and rinse under cold water to stop the cooking. Set aside.

3 Melt the butter in a 2-quart saucepan over medium heat. Add the flour and cook, whisking constantly, for about 2 minutes, until you have a roux.

4 In a small saucepan, warm the milk and, little by little, whisk it into the flour, breaking up any lumps as you go. Once all the milk has been added, cook for another minute or two until it starts to thicken. Be sure to scrape the sides.

5 Add the grated cheeses, the remaining salt, and the pepper. Stir over a low flame until all the cheese is melted and incorporated, and then pour into a serving dish.

SERVES 8

MAC & CHEESE BAKED WITH CHILI

Smoky BBQ Chili (or any leftover chili, page 98)

Leftover mac and cheese (any variety will do)

Grated cheese

. . . .

1 Preheat the oven to 350°F.

2 Place a thin layer of Smoky BBQ Chili or any leftover chili in the bottom of a casserole dish and top with leftover mac and cheese.

3 Sprinkle on some grated cheese, place in the oven, and bake for 30 to 40 minutes, until piping hot.

DEEP-FRIED MAC & CHEESE

Leftover mac and cheese (any variety will do), cold

All-purpose flour

2 large eggs whisked with ¼ cup milk

Panko (Japanese breadcrumbs)

Canola oil for deep-frying

. . . .

1 Scoop out balls of mac and cheese and drop them into the flour to coat, then into the egg wash, and then the panko.

2 Heat 4 to 5 inches of oil in a deep-fryer or heavy-bottomed stockpot to 325°F. Gently drop the mac and cheese balls into the hot oil and fry for a couple of minutes, until hot and golden. Do not overcrowd the pan. Using the deep-fryer's wire basket, a slotted spoon, or a spider, remove to paper towels to absorb extra oil or drain on a wire rack.

MAC & FOUR CHEESES

DEEP-FRIED MAC & CHEESE

CHAPTER № 11

DESSERT

WHEN YOU WERE LITTLE,

YOU USED TO HAVE TO CLEAN YOUR ENTIRE PLATE

in order to get a sweet treat at the end of the meal. Now that you're grown, you know enough to save room for—what some would contend—is the best part *of* the meal: dessert. Southerners do it right, with plenty of butter, sugar, and chocolate in their pie plates and cake pans. They also add an abundance of classic ingredients from the region, such as molasses, bourbon, pecans, key limes, and peaches.

Good Southern desserts often taste just like Grandma made them. And they also have a standalone quality to them. Some desserts are the perfect finale to a specific meal. But you can eat our Apple Crumb Pie all day long. Particularly if there's ice cream scooped alongside.

We've got all the staples, like Key Lime Pie and Peach Cobbler, in the coming pages. The cobbler dates back to when the first English settlers arrived on American soil. Due to insufficient ingredients and cooking equipment, they couldn't make their traditional pudding-style desserts, so instead they stewed a filling—typically a fruit—and topped it with a layer of scones or biscuits, pieced together. When the sweet treat cooked, the top had the appearance of a cobbled street.

There's a fantastic Pecan Pie recipe, which—if legend is to be believed—was invented by the French right after they founded New Orleans. They'd never seen the pecan before, and after the Native Americans introduced them to it, French culinary masters mixed the pecans with copious amounts of sugar and whipped up this down-home comfort food.

Also included are a few newcomer recipes that'll give the old standbys a run for their money. Like the Southern Comfort Cream Cheese Brownies and Chocolate Bourbon Pecan Torte—because liquor makes everything just a little better. We promise they're so good that thirds are often a requisite.

Desserts, particularly in the South, are another area where personal taste and family recipes often come into play. Sure, the basics for a Red Velvet Cake are always the same, but perhaps you always added a bit of beet juice for coloring (an extremely common coloring ingredient during the forties and fifties that has stuck around in recipes since then). Our recipes are guides for how we do it in our kitchen, but you can absolutely spruce up your favorite pies and cakes however you're used to making them at home. And decorative flourishes go a long way. There's no right or wrong way to do dessert, so long as the outcome is plate-licking tasty.

RED VELVET CAKE

WITH CREAM CHEESE FROSTING

This is a cake you see coming out of nearly every kitchen down South, whether it's a restaurant or Grandma's house. The cream cheese frosting is so yummy that you may have trouble getting any of it onto the cake from the bowl.

1 **Make the cake:** Preheat the oven to 350°F. Butter 3 (9-inch) cake pans and line the bottoms with parchment paper.

2 Sift the flour, sugar, baking soda, salt, and cocoa powder into a large bowl.

3 In a separate bowl, beat the oil, buttermilk, eggs, food coloring, vinegar, and vanilla.

4 Add the dry mixture to the wet mixture and stir just until combined and smooth.

5 Divide the batter evenly among the 3 pans, place in the oven, and bake for 20 to 25 minutes, until a cake tester comes out clean.

6 Place on wire racks and let cool completely in the pans while preparing the frosting.

7 **Make the cream cheese frosting:** Place the cream cheese, butter, and confectioners' sugar in the bowl of an electric mixer fitted with the whip attachment and beat at a medium speed until well combined and smooth, scraping down the sides of the bowl to break up any remaining lumps.

8 Add the vanilla, lemon juice, and salt and mix well.

9 Remove the cake layers from the pans and place 1 cake layer on a flat plate. Spoon a scant one-third of the frosting over the layer and spread it out to the sides. Place the second layer on top and spread with frosting, then repeat with the third layer, covering the sides of the cake as well.

FOR THE CAKE:

2½ cups all-purpose flour

1½ cups sugar

1 teaspoon baking soda

1 teaspoon salt

1½ teaspoons cocoa powder

1½ cups vegetable oil

1 cup buttermilk, at room temperature

2 large eggs, at room temperature

3 tablespoons red food coloring

2 teaspoons white vinegar

2 teaspoons vanilla extract

FOR THE CREAM CHEESE FROSTING:

1½ pounds cream cheese, at room temperature

1 cup (2 sticks) unsalted butter, at room temperature

2½ cups confectioners' sugar, sifted

1½ teaspoons vanilla extract

½ teaspoon fresh lemon juice

Pinch of salt

SERVES 12

SOUTHERN COMFORT
CREAM
CHEESE
BROWNIES

FOR THE BROWNIE BATTER:

8 ounces semisweet chocolate chips

½ cup (1 stick) unsalted butter

½ cup sugar

4 large eggs

1 tablespoon Southern Comfort

½ cup all-purpose flour

FOR THE CREAM CHEESE BATTER:

8 ounces cream cheese, at room temperature

½ cup sugar

2 large eggs

2½ tablespoons all-purpose flour

1 tablespoon Southern Comfort

SERVES 9

Alcohol does astoundingly well in dessert dishes, and the Southern Comfort liqueur you'll be dropping in here is no different. It gives the brownies a unique taste and a bit of a kick.

1 Preheat the oven to 350°F.

2 Spray a 9-by-9-inch baking pan with cooking spray and line it with foil so that the foil hangs over two ends. This makes it easier to remove the brownies from the pan when they are done.

3 **Make the brownie batter:** Melt the chocolate and butter in a double boiler, stirring until smooth. Remove from the heat and add the sugar.

4 Beat in the eggs one at a time until just incorporated.

5 Add the Southern Comfort and flour, but don't overmix. Pour into the prepared pan.

6 **Make the cream cheese batter:** In the bowl of an electric mixer, beat the cream cheese with the sugar until soft and smooth.

7 Add the eggs one at a time until just incorporated, then add the flour and Southern Comfort.

8 Spread on top of the brownie mixture in an even layer and, using a butter knife, swirl the batter until it starts to look marbled.

9 Place in the oven and bake for 25 minutes, or until a cake tester comes out clean.

10 Place on a wire rack and allow to cool completely in the pan before cutting.

APPLE CRUMB PIE

We like to use some sweet apples and some tart apples for this pie. Our apples of choice are Granny Smith and Empire, McIntosh, or Gala. One trick here is that each component can be prepared a day in advance and then assembled and baked the day you plan to serve it.

1 Preheat the oven to 350°F.

2 **Make the pie filling:** In a large bowl, combine all the ingredients for the pie filling and put them in a baking dish. Cover with aluminum foil and bake for about 30 minutes. When it comes out of the oven, stir it well and let it cool. (This step may be done the day before.) Keep the oven on if you are proceeding with the recipe.

3 Roll the pie dough out and fit it into a 10-inch pie plate, crimping the edges however you like. Place in the refrigerator until ready to use.

4 Line the pie shell with parchment paper or aluminum foil and fill with baking weights, dry beans, or rice. Bake the shell for about 15 minutes, until it sets up. Remove the paper or foil and weights.

5 **Make the crumb topping:** Combine the ingredients for the crumb topping in the bowl of a food processor or a mixer and combine until crumbs start to form. Take care not to overmix, or you will have a mass of dough.

6 Place the cooled filling in the pie shell and cover with the crumb topping. Bake for 30 to 40 minutes, until the topping is set and the filling starts bubbling around the edges. Let the pie sit at room temperature until cool.

FOR THE PIE FILLING:

7 cups peeled, cored, and thinly sliced apples

¼ cup light brown sugar

1 tablespoon cornstarch

¾ teaspoon ground cinnamon

¼ teaspoon ground ginger

⅛ teaspoon ground nutmeg

1½ teaspoons fresh lemon juice

1½ teaspoons vanilla extract

2 tablespoons unsalted butter, melted

1 recipe Pie Dough (page 242)

FOR THE CRUMB TOPPING:

1 cup all-purpose flour

⅓ cup light brown sugar

⅓ cup granulated sugar

1 teaspoon ground cinnamon

½ cup (1 stick) unsalted butter, diced and chilled

SERVES 8

KEY LIME PIE

A creamy slice of this pie is a solid dessert for any occasion. The sweetened condensed milk helps give it that silky smooth texture that keeps forks coming back for more.

FOR THE GRAHAM CRACKER PIE CRUST:

1 cup graham cracker crumbs (or 1 packet of graham crackers ground to a fine crumb in a food processor)

¼ cup sugar

½ cup (1 stick) unsalted butter, melted

FOR THE FILLING:

4 large egg yolks

1 (14-ounce) can sweetened condensed milk

½ cup key lime juice

½ teaspoon cream of tartar

SERVES 6

1 Preheat the oven to 350°F.

2 **Make the crust:** In a large bowl, combine the graham cracker crumbs, sugar, and butter (it will look like wet sand) and press into a 9-inch pie plate.

3 Refrigerate for 15 minutes, then place in the oven and bake for 10 minutes, until if you slightly shake the pan, the center appears firm, not loose.

4 **Make the filling:** In a large bowl, whisk together the egg yolks and sweetened condensed milk.

5 Whisk in the key lime juice and cream of tartar.

6 Pour into the pie shell and bake for 15 minutes, or until set.

7 Remove from the oven and cool on a wire rack for 10 minutes, then cover and refrigerate. Serve cold.

CHOCOLATE BOURBON
PECAN TORTE

If you don't want to bother with the ganache, you don't have to—a simple dusting of cocoa powder will do. Though with that extra bit of bourbon . . . need we say more?

1 Preheat the oven to 350°F and butter and flour a 10-inch springform pan.

2 **Make the cake:** In a food processor, process the pecans with ¼ cup of the sugar and the salt until the mixture is very fine.

3 Melt the chocolate with the butter in the top part of a double boiler over barely simmering water, stirring until smooth.

4 Remove the bowl from the heat and sift the cocoa power over the melted chocolate; mix well. Add the nut mixture and stir to combine.

5 On the bowl of an electric mixer, whisk the eggs with the remaining 1¼ cups sugar. Place the mixture in a double boiler over simmering water. Continue whisking until the sugar dissolves. Return the bowl to the mixer and beat on high speed until the eggs triple in volume. Add the bourbon.

6 Gently fold the eggs into the chocolate mixture in three additions.

7 Pour the batter into the prepared pan and bake for 35 to 40 minutes, or when you can stick a toothpick in the center and it comes out clean.

8 Let the cake cool in the pan on a wire rack.

9 **Make the bourbon ganache:** While the cake is cooling, place the chocolate in a heatproof bowl. Heat the cream to scalding and pour it over the chocolate. Let it sit for 5 minutes without stirring.

10 Add the butter and whisk to combine. Add the bourbon. Let the ganache sit for another 5 to 10 minutes, until it thickens slightly.

11 Carefully remove the sides of the pan from the cooled cake. Pour the ganache over the top of the cake, spreading it all over and along the sides.

FOR THE CAKE:

1 cup pecan halves

1½ cups sugar

¼ teaspoon salt

16 ounces bittersweet chocolate (chips, chunks, or chopped)

1 cup (2 sticks) unsalted butter

5 tablespoons cocoa powder

7 large eggs

1 tablespoon good-quality bourbon

FOR THE BOURBON GANACHE:

16 ounces bittersweet chocolate (chips, chunks, or chopped)

1 cup heavy cream

2 tablespoons unsalted butter

1 tablespoon good-quality bourbon (you'll taste the liquor more because it doesn't cook off)

SERVES 12 to 16

PEACH COBBLER

6 cups thick peach slices or chunks

1 teaspoon grated lemon zest

½ cup plus 2 to 3 tablespoons sugar, depending on the sweetness of peaches

2 tablespoons cornstarch

⅛ teaspoon ground nutmeg

2 teaspoons vanilla extract

¾ cup (1½ sticks) unsalted butter, softened

2 cups all-purpose flour

2 tablespoons baking powder

¼ teaspoon salt

1 large egg

¾ cup milk

Cinnamon and sugar for sprinkling (optional)

SERVES 6 to 8

Bubbling, hot, fragrant peaches get cobbled here. Be sure to hit it with a scoop of vanilla ice cream when plating.

1 Preheat the oven to 350°F and butter a 2-quart baking dish.

2 In a large bowl, toss the peaches with the lemon zest, 2 to 3 tablespoons of sugar, the cornstarch, nutmeg, and 1 teaspoon of the vanilla. Pour into the baking dish.

3 In the bowl of an electric mixer, using the paddle attachment, beat the butter with the remaining ½ cup of sugar until light and fluffy.

4 In a separate bowl, combine the flour, baking powder, and salt.

5 In a third bowl, whisk together the egg, milk, and the remaining 1 teaspoon of vanilla.

6 Add the flour mixture to the butter mixture, then add the milk mixture; it will not be a smooth batter.

7 Spread the batter on top of the peaches. If you like, you can sprinkle a little cinnamon and sugar on top.

8 Place in the oven and bake for 40 to 50 minutes, until the top is golden brown and it's bubbling at the sides of the pan. Let cool for 15 to 20 minutes but no longer—it is best served warm.

S'MORES BARS

Everyone loves s'mores, and this recipe brings enough of the campfire indoors to satisfy kids of all ages.

½ cup (1 stick) unsalted butter, melted

3 cups graham cracker crumbs (or 3 packets of graham crackers ground to a fine crumb in a food processor)

1 cup semisweet chocolate chips

2 cups mini marshmallows

1 (14-ounce) can sweetened condensed milk

SERVES 9

1 Preheat the oven to 350°F and butter a 9-by-9-inch square baking pan.

2 In a small bowl, combine the melted butter with 2 cups of the graham cracker crumbs. Press the crumb mixture into the bottom of the pan.

3 Spread the chocolate chips on top of the crumb crust, followed by the marshmallows.

4 Pour the condensed milk evenly over the chips and marshmallows.

5 Sprinkle the remaining 1 cup of graham cracker crumbs on top and place into the oven.

6 Bake for 20 to 30 minutes, until the marshmallows start to puff and the condensed milk turns golden in spots.

7 Place on a wire rack and cool completely, then cut into squares.

BROWN SUGAR BANANA BREAD PUDDING

8 cups cubed crustless bread

4 large eggs

2 cups milk

1 cup plus 3 tablespoons heavy cream

1¼ cups brown sugar

1 tablespoon vanilla extract

⅛ teaspoon ground nutmeg

½ teaspoon fresh lemon juice

5 bananas, cut into 1-inch slices

SERVES 8

This a great use for leftover or stale bread. We like to use a chewy Italian-type loaf for this dessert.

1 Preheat the oven to 325°F and butter a 2½- to 3-quart baking dish.

2 Place the cubed bread on a baking sheet and bake for about 15 minutes, until toasted.

3 In a large bowl, beat together the eggs, milk, 1 cup of the heavy cream, 1 cup of the brown sugar, the vanilla, and nutmeg. When the bread comes out of the oven, let it cool for 5 to 10 minutes, then add it to the bowl, stir to coat, and let it soak for 15 minutes.

4 Meanwhile, heat the remaining ¼ cup brown sugar with the lemon juice in a large sauté pan; when the sugar starts to melt, add the remaining 3 tablespoons of heavy cream to make it like a caramel sauce. Add the banana to the caramel and mix well. Remove from the heat.

5 Put about half of the soaked bread into the baking dish and top with the banana mixture. Pour the remaining bread and any remaining liquid evenly on top of the bananas.

6 Place in the oven and bake for 30 to 40 minutes, until set. Spoon it into a bowl or plate and serve warm.

CHOCOLATE PEANUT BUTTER CAKE

Reese's got it right when they decided to mix chocolate and peanut butter together, as we did with this cake. All it needs is a tall glass of ice-cold milk.

1 Preheat the oven to 350°F. Butter 2 (10-by-2-inch) cake pans, line them with parchment, and dust with flour.

2 **Make the cake:** In a large bowl, whisk together the boiling water and cocoa powder until it is smooth and lump free. Whisk in the cold water.

3 Sift the flour, baking soda, baking powder, and salt into a large bowl.

4 In the bowl of an electric mixer, beat together the butter and sugar until light and fluffy.

5 Add the eggs one at a time, mixing after each addition. Scrape down the sides of the bowl and add the vanilla.

6 Add the dry ingredients in 3 additions alternating with the cocoa powder mixture. Mix until smooth.

7 Divide the batter between the 2 pans, place in the oven, and bake for 20 to 25 minutes. Place pans on wire racks to cool completely.

8 **Make the peanut butter buttercream:** In the bowl of an electric mixer, beat the peanut butter, butter, and cream cheese until smooth and lump free. Add the confectioners' sugar and vanilla and beat until smooth.

9 To assemble, place a layer bottom-side up on a flat cake plate. Remove the parchment paper. Spread about one-third of the frosting on top. Place the second layer on top, bottom-side up, remove the parchment paper, and spread the remaining frosting evenly on the top and the sides of the cake.

FOR THE CAKE:

1 cup boiling water

1 cup cocoa powder

1 cup cold water

3 cups cake flour

2 teaspoons baking soda

½ teaspoon baking powder

¾ teaspoon salt

1 cup (2 sticks) unsalted butter, at room temperature

2½ cups sugar

4 large eggs

1½ teaspoons vanilla extract

FOR THE PEANUT BUTTER BUTTERCREAM:

1½ cups smooth peanut butter, at room temperature

1 cup (2 sticks) unsalted butter, at room temperature

4 ounces cream cheese, at room temperature

¾ cup confectioners' sugar, sifted

1 teaspoon vanilla extract

SERVES 12

PECAN PIE

1 recipe Pie Dough (page 242)

½ cup brown sugar

4 tablespoons (½ stick) unsalted butter, melted

¼ cup corn syrup

¾ cup maple syrup

Pinch of salt

1 teaspoon vanilla extract

2 cups pecan halves

SERVES 6 to 8

Sweet, sticky, and nutty, pecan pie is the all-time iconic Southern dessert. Substitute bourbon for the vanilla if there are no kids around. Or just tell them this pie is for the adults only.

1 Preheat the oven to 375°F.

2 Roll out the pie dough and lay it in a 10-inch pie plate. Trim the dough, leaving a 1-inch overhang. Fold the extra dough under so it covers the rim of the plate, forming a decorative edge. Refrigerate or freeze the dough for 30 minutes.

3 Line the pie shell with parchment paper or aluminum foil and fill with baking weights, dry beans, or rice. Bake the shell for about 15 minutes, until it sets up. Remove the paper or foil and weights.

4 While the pie shell is baking, combine the brown sugar, butter, corn syrup, maple syrup, salt, and vanilla in a large bowl, and mix until well incorporated. Add the pecans.

5 Pour the filling into the pie shell, place in the oven, and bake for 25 to 35 minutes, until the edges are slightly puffed. If the edges start to brown, wrap aluminum foil around the edges of the crust to prevent burning.

6 Cool completely before cutting.

BUTTERMILK PIE

1 recipe Pie Dough (below)

FOR THE FILLING:

1½ cups sugar

¾ teaspoon ground cinnamon

¼ teaspoon ground nutmeg

2 tablespoons cornstarch

1 teaspoon vanilla extract

½ cup (1 stick) unsalted butter, melted

3 large eggs, at room temperature

1 cup buttermilk, at room temperature

SERVES 8

This sweet Southern pie is perfect with a spoonful of fresh berries served alongside.

1 Preheat the oven to 300°F.

2 Roll out the pie dough and lay it in a 10-inch pie plate. Trim the dough, leaving a 1-inch overhang. Fold the extra dough under so it covers the rim of the plate, forming a decorative edge. Refrigerate or freeze the dough for 30 minutes.

3 In a large bowl, whisk together all the ingredients for the filling except the buttermilk.

4 Add the buttermilk and pour into the unbaked pie shell.

5 Place in the oven and bake for about 50 minutes, until a small, thin knife inserted through the center comes out clean. Cool to room temperature, then cover and refrigerate until ready to serve.

PIE DOUGH

1½ cups all-purpose flour

½ teaspoon sugar

⅛ teaspoon salt

½ cup (1 stick) unsalted butter, diced and chilled

1 large egg yolk

3 to 5 tablespoons ice water

This recipe makes enough dough for one 10-inch pie crust.

1 Combine the flour, sugar salt, and butter in the bowl of an electric mixer and mix on medium speed until it resembles coarse crumbs.

2 In a small bowl, whisk the egg yolk with 3 tablespoons of the water and add to the flour mixture. Add the remaining water, 1 tablespoon at a time, if necessary to form a crumbly dough.

3 Turn the dough out and mix in any flour remaining at the bottom of the bowl with a few quick kneading motions to bring it together into a ball—don't overwork the dough or it will not be tender.

4 Form into a disc, wrap in plastic wrap, and refrigerate for 1 hour to rest.

BROWNIE SUNDAE

WITH HOT FUDGE SAUCE

We serve these with butterscotch swirl ice cream, but you may use your favorite ice cream flavor—just have plenty of it. Topped with homemade hot fudge sauce, it's an understatement to say that this is a crowd pleaser.

1 Preheat the oven to 325°F. Butter a 9-by-9-inch square pan.

2 **Make the brownies:** Sift the flour, baking soda, and salt into a large bowl and set aside.

3 In the top portion of a double boiler over barely simmering water, melt the butter with the chocolate, stirring until smooth.

4 Remove from the heat and mix in the sugars.

5 Add the eggs one at a time, mixing to incorporate after each addition.

6 Add 2 tablespoons of water and the vanilla.

7 Add the dry ingredients and stir until just incorporated. Scrape into the prepared pan and bake for 30 to 40 minutes, until a cake tester comes out with a little crumb.

8 **Make the hot fudge sauce:** While the brownies are baking, combine the cocoa powder with the sugars in a heavy-bottomed 1- or 2-quart pot. Add the remaining ingredients and whisk until smooth and lump free. Keep warm.

9 Let the brownies cool off before cutting. Cut into 9 squares (or portion how you like). Place a scoop of your favorite ice cream on top of the brownie and then drizzle some warm sauce on top. Finish it off with a little whipped cream and a maraschino cherry (or just dig in after the sauce is on!).

FOR THE BROWNIES:

1 cup plus 2 tablespoons all-purpose flour

¼ teaspoon baking soda

¼ teaspoon salt

½ cup (1 stick) unsalted butter

8 ounces bittersweet chocolate, chopped

½ cup light brown sugar

½ cup granulated sugar

2 large eggs

1 teaspoon vanilla extract

FOR THE HOT FUDGE SAUCE:

½ cup cocoa powder

½ cup granulated sugar

½ cup brown sugar

¼ cup (½ stick) unsalted butter, melted

6 ounces evaporated milk

⅛ teaspoon salt

¼ cup semisweet chocolate chips

½ teaspoon vanilla extract

★

Ice cream for topping

Whipped cream for topping (optional)

Maraschino cherries for topping (optional)

SERVES 9

BOOKS
FOR FURTHER READING

These are books that we think do a good job of explaining barbecue methods, equipment, and iconic Southern dishes that accompany 'cue:

Biscuits, Spoonbread, and Sweet Potato Pie by Bill Neal

Fanny Flagg's Original Whistle Stop Cafe Cookbook: Featuring Fried Green Tomatoes, Southern Barbecue, Banana Split Cake, and Many Other Great Recipes by Fanny Flagg

The Gift of Southern Cooking: Recipes and Revelations from Two Great American Cooks by Edna Lewis and Scott Peacock

Holy Smoke: The Big Book of North Carolina Barbecue by John Shelton Reed and Dale Volberg Reed

The Kansas City Barbecue Society Cookbook by Ardie Davis, Paul Kirk, and Carolyn Wells

Legends of Texas Barbecue Cookbook by Robb Walsh

Low & Slow: Master the Art of Barbecue in 5 Easy Lessons by Gary Wiviott

Peace, Love, and Barbecue: Recipes, Secrets, Tall Tales, and Outright Lies from the Legends of Barbecue by Mike Mills and Amy Mills Tunnicliffe

Smoke and Spice: Cooking with Smoke, the Real Way to Barbecue by Cheryl and Bill Jamison

Smokin' with Myron Mixon: Recipes Made Simple from the Winningest Man in Barbecue by Myron Mixon

Southern Food: At Home, on the Road, in History by John Egerton

CONVERSION CHARTS

WEIGHT EQUIVALENTS

The metric weights given in this chart are not exact equivalents, but have been rounded up or down slightly to make measuring easier.

AVOIRDUPOIS	METRIC
¼ oz	7 g
½ oz	15 g
1 oz	30 g
2 oz	60 g
3 oz	90 g
4 oz	115 g
5 oz	150 g
6 oz	175 g
7 oz	200 g
8 oz (½ lb)	225 g
9 oz	250 g
10 oz	300 g
11 oz	325 g
12 oz	350 g
13 oz	375 g
14 oz	400 g
15 oz	425 g
16 oz (1 lb)	450 g
1½ lb	750 g
2 lb	900 g
2¼ lb	1 kg
3 lb	1.4 kg
4 lb	1.8 kg

VOLUME EQUIVALENTS

These are not exact equivalents for American cups and spoons, but have been rounded up or down slightly to make measuring easier.

AMERICAN	METRIC	IMPERIAL
¼ tsp	1.2 ml	
½ tsp	2.5 ml	
1 tsp	5.0 ml	
½ Tbsp (1.5 tsp)	7.5 ml	
1 Tbsp (3 tsp)	15 ml	
¼ cup (4 Tbsp)	60 ml	2 fl oz
⅓ cup (5 Tbsp)	75 ml	2.5 fl oz
½ cup (8 Tbsp)	125 ml	4 fl oz
⅔ cup (10 Tbsp)	150 ml	5 fl oz
¾ cup (12 Tbsp)	175 ml	6 fl oz
1 cup (16 Tbsp)	250 ml	8 fl oz
1¼ cups	300 ml	10 fl oz (½ pint)
1½ cups	350 ml	12 fl oz
2 cups (1 pint)	500 ml	16 fl oz
2½ cups	625 ml	20 fl oz (1 pint)
1 quart	1 liter	32 fl oz

OVEN MARK	F	C	GAS
Very cool	250–275	130–140	½–1
Cool	300	150	2
Warm	325	170	3
Moderate	350	180	4
Moderately hot	375–400	190–200	5–6
Hot	425–450	220–230	7–8
Very hot	475	250	9

ALL-PURPOSE FLOUR

It's critical to weigh certain ingredients for successful baking. Dry ingredients—especially flour—compress easily into a cup measure, making the scoop-and-level method inaccurate. The most accurate way to measure flour is to weigh it after sifting. Here are the weight equivalents for common volume measurements of all-purpose flour.

WEIGHT	VOLUME
1 ounce	3 tablespoons
2 ounces	¼ cup + 2 tablespoons
3 ounces	½ cup + 1 tablespoon
4 ounces	¾ cup + ½ teaspoon
5 ounces	1 cup
6 ounces	1 cup + 1 tablespoon
7 ounces	1¼ cups + 2 tablespoons
8 ounces	1½ cups + 1 tablespoon
9 ounces	1¾ cups + ½ teaspoon
10 ounces	2 cups
11 ounces	2 cups + 1 tablespoon
12 ounces	2¼ cups + 2 tablespoons
12½ ounces	2½ cups
13 ounces	2½ cups + 1 tablespoon
13½ ounces	2½ cups + 3 tablespoons
14 ounces	2¾ cups + ½ teaspoon
14½ ounces	2¾ cups + 1 tablespoon +1 teaspoon
15 ounces	3 cups

SUPERFINE GRANULATED SUGAR

Superfine granulated sugar, the sugar generally used in this book, weighs about 8 ounces per cup. (Standard table sugar, or typical granulated sugar, weighs 7 ounces per cup. It has a larger crystal than extra-fine granulated, so less mass fits into a one-cup measure.)

WEIGHT	VOLUME
1 ounce	2 tablespoons
2 ounces	¼ cup
3 ounces	6 tablespoons
4 ounces	½ cup
5 ounces	½ cup + 2 tablespoons
6 ounces	¾ cup
7 ounces	¾ cup + 2 tablespoons
8 ounces	1 cup
12 ounces	1½ cups
16 ounces	2 cups
20 ounces	2½ cups
24 ounces	3 cups

OTHER INGREDIENTS

INGREDIENT	WEIGHT	VOLUME
butter	4 ounces	8 tablespoons (1 stick)
confectioners' sugar	4¼ ounces	1 cup

INDEX

Note: Page references in *italic* refer to illustrations.

ACKNOWLEDGMENTS

WHEN I FIRST SET FOOT IN BROTHER JIMMY'S IN 1996, THE SEEDS OF INSPIRATION FOR THIS BOOK WERE PLANTED.

Over the past fifteen years, countless people passing through our doors, from employees to customers to friends, have helped shape much of what has been captured in this book. The goal of this book was to try to embody as much of the fun, camaraderie, and cheer—and, of course, food—that has been, and always will be, essential parts of the Brother Jimmy's experience. Without the years of hard work by the entire staff, as well as the passionate dedication of our fans, we would not be what we are today.

For years I've wanted to produce a book that would convey the essence of Brother Jimmy's, and a ton of work had to be put into the process in order to achieve this final product. A special thanks goes to my sister and executive chef, Eva Pesantez. For almost three years we have been sorting through this process and without Eva's dedication and talent it would have been impossible. I'd also like to thank our writer, Sean Evans, whose dedication to this project enabled us to beautifully capture the texture of the Brother Jimmy's experience.

In addition I'd like to thank David Getraer and Jon Kachejian for their support while I was focusing on other things, such as this book. Thank you as well to Eric Lupfer at WME for finding me such a great publisher, and Natalie Kaire and Elinor Hutton from Stewart, Tabori & Chang, who understood what I wanted to achieve from the very beginning. The book would not have been the same had they not been involved.

And, of course, I'd like to thank Jimmy Goldman for getting me into this business in the first place.

JOSH LEBOWITZ, OWNER AND PRESIDENT OF BROTHER JIMMY'S, has been having a love affair with barbecue since college, inspired from a young age by the regional BBQ cultures of the United States. In the last ten years, under Lebowitz's ownership, Brother Jimmy's has grown from a few tiny BBQ shacks to six insanely popular NYC-based restaurants and bars, as well as franchises in Puerto Rico and St. Martin, a bustling catering business, a concession at Yankee Stadium, and a full line of supermarket-ready products. Lebowitz lives in New York.

LUCY SCHAEFFER regularly shoots food, lifestyle, and kids stories for magazines such as *Parents*, *Food & Wine*, *Martha Stewart Living*, and *Everyday with Rachael Ray*. She has photographed twenty-four cookbooks and doesn't plan to stop until she's sampled every possible combination of foods. Lucy lives in Brooklyn with her husband and young daughter.